Making Sense of Kant's "Critique of Pure Reason"

Making Sense of Kant's "Critique of Pure Reason"

A Philosophical Introduction

Michael Pendlebury

BLOOMSBURY ACADEMIC
LONDON · NEW YORK · OXFORD · NEW DELHI · SYDNEY

BLOOMSBURY ACADEMIC
Bloomsbury Publishing Plc
50 Bedford Square, London, WC1B 3DP, UK
1385 Broadway, New York, NY 10018, USA
29 Earlsfort Terrace, Dublin 2, Ireland

BLOOMSBURY, BLOOMSBURY ACADEMIC and the Diana logo are trademarks
of Bloomsbury Publishing Plc

First published in Great Britain 2022

Series design by Irene Martinez Costa

A catalogue record for this book is available from the British Library.

A catalog record for this book is available from the Library of Congress.

ISBN: HB: 978-1-3502-5476-3
PB: 978-1-3502-5477-0
ePDF: 978-1-3502-5478-7
eBook: 978-1-3502-5479-4

Typeset by Deanta Global Publishing Services, Chennai, India
Printed and bound in Great Britain

To find out more about our authors and books visit www.bloomsbury.com and
sign up for our newsletters.

CONTENTS

PREFACE

Kant's *Critique of Pure Reason*, which is one of the greatest works of the Enlightenment, has had, and continues to have, an enormous impact on modern philosophy. But it is a very long and difficult work that is not accessible to many of those with a potential interest in it. The overall purpose of this short book is to help make Kant's thinking in the *Critique of Pure Reason* more accessible to a wider range of readers. This is not to suggest that it is an easy read. No book that seriously attempts to make sense of the *Critique of Pure Reason* could be.

The book is designed primarily for two uses. One is to serve as a freestanding introduction to and selective overview of the *Critique* for those who would like to learn more about it, including educated general readers, students with philosophical interests, students who are considering taking a course on the *Critique*, and students who are preparing for or taking such a course. The other is to serve as a supplementary textbook for use in text-based courses on the *Critique* or courses that cover significant material from the *Critique*. Some suggestions to readers and instructors on how to use the book appear immediately after this Preface.

It may seem surprising that I am offering such a short guide to a book as long as Kant's *Critique of Pure Reason*, but it is no accident. Those who are approaching or tackling the *Critique* for the first time need guidance on a few crucially important things: the major claims Kant makes in the *Critique*, how they hang together, and how Kant supports them; the way in which his most important reasoning unfolds over the course of the *Critique*; and some of the major interpretive disagreements between different approaches to the *Critique*. These aspects of the big picture must, of course, be backed up by enough attention to detail at key points to help a new reader get through the most important sections of the *Critique* without succumbing to utter confusion. A shorter book is an appropriate instrument to accomplish these goals because excessive attention to too many passages in the *Critique* that seem puzzling, cryptic, ambiguous, enigmatic, or opaque—or to too many detailed interpretive questions about specific points—is likely to distract, discourage, and overwhelm someone who is new to the *Critique*.

My approach to Kant is sympathetic. Focusing on the most important parts of the text of the second edition of the *Critique of Pure Reason*, I seek to provide a clear and intelligible account of this remarkable work, concentrating on matters which I take to be of ongoing philosophical interest. Among the most important reasons for reading great works in the history of philosophy, such as the *Critique*, is that they are relevant to current philosophical concerns. And perhaps the most important reason why undergraduates in philosophy should be expected to study such works is to give them access to an unsurpassable bounty of philosophical ideas, tools, successes, and failures, which should enhance their philosophical understanding and skills regardless of the particular topics in philosophy in which they become most interested.

My guiding assumptions in the book are that Kant is and must be understood as a humanist; that his reasoning in the *Critique* is driven largely by an interest in human knowledge and the cognitive capacities that make it possible; and that he is not a skeptic but accepts that human beings have objective knowledge and seeks to explain how this is possible. I offer an integrated account of the way in which Kant does this that emerges progressively over the course of the book. My central goal is to help those who are new to the *Critique* make sense of it. In order to do this, I follow one main line of interpretation rather than discussing a range of possibilities at every turn. Where possible, I tend to favor readings that attribute views to Kant that are more likely to be acceptable to educated and scientifically literate readers. Some commentators may disparage such an approach as "anodyne,"[1] but if it engages those who are new to the *Critique* and helps put them in a position to explore alternative readings, it will have done a very useful job.

For those in the know, I should say something about my interpretation—or, more accurately, my reconstruction—of the *Critique*. Kant is sometimes understood as committed to a position which he explicitly disavows, namely, subjectivist idealism, or some variant thereof. In contrast, I interpret him as a moderate realist who is committed to objects which are independent of us, but who holds that these objects must conform to certain *a priori* aspects of our cognition if it is to be possible for them to serve as objects of experience about which we can have empirical knowledge. So Kant's transcendental idealism, as I understand it, is the view that these *a priori* aspects of our cognition are (in his words) "conditions of the possibility of experience" which independent objects must satisfy in order for us to be able to cognize them. Some aspects of the way in which I develop this sort of interpretation are novel and may therefore be of interest to more advanced students, teachers, and scholars of the *Critique of Pure Reason*. But those who are acquainted with the secondary literature on the *Critique* should be warned that, because of the length of the book and the fact that it is not aimed primarily at Kant scholars, I do not defend the details of my interpretation against many possible scholarly objections. On the other hand, one of the great advantages of a short book on the *Critique* is that it can do a better job of capturing and displaying the unity of a particular interpretation.

In any case, as I say in Chapter 1, I do not claim to offer the best interpretation of the *Critique*, but only to present an intelligible and accessible interpretation that can provide a useful starting point for further work. I hope my interpretation will not deter instructors who support other interpretations from considering this introduction as a supplementary textbook, because it can be pedagogically useful for instructors to contrast their own interpretation with an alternative interpretation to which their students have easy access, and to illustrate the strengths of their own by showing how it avoids the problems of the alternative.

This book is distinctive in some respects, including the following. First, I tackle the Principles (with a focus on the Analogies and the Second Postulate) before the Transcendental Deduction. I do this because Kant's thinking in the Principles is much more accessible; because it helps those who are new to the *Critique* get a handle on the nature of Kant's project; and because it prepares the ground for the much more challenging Transcendental Deduction. But (as indicated in the section "How to Use This Book") this unusual order of presentation does not mean that the book cannot serve as an effective guide in courses that follow other orders, including the order of the *Critique* itself. Second, I pay far more attention than the authors of most introductory books on the *Critique* to Kant's treatment of imagination and imaginative synthesis in the Analytic, because of the crucial role which they play in his account of cognition and in his reasoning in the second stage of the Transcendental Deduction in B. Third, I postpone presenting considered statements of my accounts of Kant's transcendental idealism and his talk about things in themselves until the last chapter on the ground that these are highly controversial issues that depend upon the interpretation of many other things in the *Critique* that should not be second-guessed.

I give proportionally more space to the Analytic than to the Aesthetic and the Dialectic because I think that the Analytic is not only the heart of the *Critique* but also because the essential material in it is most difficult to understand, especially for a new reader. Some may be surprised that I include only one chapter on the Dialectic, but it is the longest chapter and it constitutes about 20 percent of the main text of the book. This is in line with the space devoted to the Dialectic in most recent English introductions to the *Critique*. (I know of only one recent introduction that devotes proportionally more space to the dialectic, viz., about 27 percent.) I deal with the Dialectic in a single chapter because this allows for a more integrated treatment of the material in it that I see as most important for a basic understanding of the *Critique*.

I have taught a course on Kant's *Critique of Pure Reason* to undergraduates on at least twenty occasions at the University of the Witwatersrand ("Wits") and North Carolina State University over the past thirty-two years. I am very grateful to all the students who have taken this course for giving me the opportunity to try to help them make sense of the *Critique*. This has taught me much more about it than I could have learned in any other way.

I am also grateful to all those in academic philosophy who have, over the years, influenced and helped me develop my philosophical views—through discussion, responses to my work, and their own work. I will not try to list them, because I could not succeed. But I do have two specific acknowledgments. I am grateful to Carl Posy for allowing me to audit his basic graduate course on the *Critique of Pure Reason* at Duke University while I was on sabbatical leave at the University of North Carolina at Chapel Hill in 1995–6—especially because it was in this course that I discovered the benefits of tackling the Analogies before the Transcendental Deduction. And I am grateful to Paul Voice for inviting me to present a seminar on the Transcendental Deduction in his course on the *Critique* at Bennington College in October 2012. I began to develop the interpretation of

the Deduction presented in Chapter 6 for that seminar and I was
delighted to discuss my thoughts with an extraordinarily enthusiastic
and well-prepared group of undergraduates.

I am especially grateful to Bloomsbury's reviewers for a number
of suggestions that have led to significant improvements and to my
commissioning editor, Jade Grogan, for his support, understanding,
and flexibility. Most of all, I am grateful to my partner in life, Mary
Tjiattas, and our son, Thomas Pendlebury, both of whom drew
my attention to useful passages in Kant's corpus and to significant
material in the secondary literature. Both of them also read the
whole of a near-final draft of the manuscript and saved me from
many errors. But over the years they have also done very much more.

Thomas (T. A. Pendlebury) started to develop a serious interest
in the *Critique* after becoming a graduate student in philosophy at
Harvard in 2014, and his PhD dissertation, which he submitted in
2020, was on the *Critique*. Thomas and I have been engaged in an
intermittent but ongoing discussion about the *Critique* for several
years. Fed by his work in progress and my work on this book,
this discussion has become increasingly interesting and useful. I
have learned an enormous amount from it, and it has led to many
improvements in the book.

In 1989, before Mary and I were together, I was given the task
of teaching the *Critique* for the first time. Because of my lack of
expertise, I was wondering how to manage it. Mary, who had taught
the *Critique* at Wits a couple of times as a leave replacement and
was then teaching in the Department of Education while working
on a PhD in philosophy, heard about my plight and offered to help
me teach the *Critique* on top of her regular duties. Hardly believing
my good fortune, I seized the opportunity. Without having Mary
as a co-teacher, I would never have managed, especially because
the material she covered included the Transcendental Deduction,
which I found utterly opaque. My share included the Aesthetic
and the Analogies, which I found much more accessible, and the
Schematism, which was short enough to wrestle with. I will always
be grateful to Mary for my easy introduction to the teaching of
the *Critique*, without which I might never have wanted to teach
it again or to explore it in greater depth; for subsequently sharing
her life with me and enriching mine; for endless philosophical
discussion; and for her help with this book, which I dedicate to
her.

HOW TO USE
THIS BOOK

This book could be read as a freestanding introduction to the *Critique of Pure Reason* by anyone who would like to discover what Kant is up to in his great masterpiece, or who would like to try to make sense of his views and arguments—whether out of sheer intellectual curiosity or as part of a program of study. It could also serve as a taster for students who are considering taking a course on the *Critique*, as an additional resource or a supplementary textbook for students taking a text-based course on the *Critique*, as a refresher for those who have previously read the *Critique*, or as a source of ideas on how to understand or teach it.

For most readers who are not engaged in a course on the *Critique* and who are either not acquainted with it or want a refresher, it would be best to read this book in the order in which the chapters and sections are presented, because later material often presupposes and builds upon earlier material. For the same reason, those who are acquainted with the *Critique* and wish to dip into later parts of the book to discover what I have to say about a particular topic may find that this depends upon material covered earlier. If so, they should be able to identify the places in which I discuss that material with the help of my frequent cross-references and the overview of my interpretation of Kant's account of synthetic *a priori* knowledge presented in Section 7.4. (Those who are new to the *Critique* should, however, be warned that this overview will not be accessible before they have read most of Chapters 2–6.)

I turn now to the needs of instructors who are preparing courses that are on the *Critique* or include a significant amount of material from it. There is a wide variation in the material which such instructors can reasonably cover and deal with in detail, depending not only on the amount of time available but also on other factors such as their teaching styles, writing assignments, and judgments about what is most important in the *Critique*. In a regular one-semester course in an American public university (which involves a total of thirty-two to thirty-five hours in the classroom over fourteen weeks, during which typical full-time students take the equivalent of at least four further courses of the same weight), I have managed to cover most of the material dealt with in Chapters 2–5 and Sections 6.1–6.4 in detail and to squeeze in some of the remaining material at the end. On one fortuitous occasion, I was able to include a quick treatment of material dealt with in Section 6.5, Chapter 7, and Sections 8.1, 8.3, 8.5, 8.6, 8.9, and 9.1 during the last two-and-a-half weeks. I could have done so more often if I'd had a book like this one as a supplementary text. Given half the class time, I would aim to cover most of the material dealt with in Chapters 2–5 in detail. Other instructors could reasonably aim to cover less material in the *Critique* in greater depth or more material in less depth.

In addition to serving as a general guide for students, this book can be used to facilitate each of these two approaches to teaching it. In the case of the first, it can help the students bridge the gaps between the selections from the *Critique* that they study in depth in class; in the case of the second, it can help them come to grips with the material that is covered in less depth in class. The book has been prepared so that it is possible for students to read only sections corresponding to the material covered in a course in any reasonable order selected by the instructor—with occasional supplementary reading from earlier sections identified with the help of cross-references or the overview in Section 7.4. Yet I think that it would facilitate teaching to have students read most of the book up to the sections dealing with material to be covered at a particular stage of the course beforehand. For instance, in courses in which the Transcendental Deduction is (as usual) taught before the Principles, I believe that most students will be able to make better sense of the Deduction if they read Chapter 5 (without necessarily reading the Principles chapter in the *Critique*) in advance, so that they are aware of what the Deduction will lead to.

NOTE ON CITATIONS OF AND QUOTATIONS FROM KANT'S WORKS

Following standard practice, I cite passages in Kant's *Critique of Pure Reason* in parentheses using the pagination of the original versions preceded by the letter "A" in the case of the first edition (1781) and the letter "B" in the case of the second (1787), and I give both citations in the case of passages that are common to the two editions. This pagination is indicated in most reputable versions of the *Critique*, typically in the margins.

Three highly respected translations of the *Critique of Pure Reason* are often quoted in recent work in English. The first is the translation by Norman Kemp Smith, which was originally published by Macmillan in 1929 and reissued with corrections in 1933, and is now available with an introduction by Howard Caygill and a bibliography by Gary Banham (London: Palgrave Macmillan, 2007). Kemp Smith's translation is superbly fluent but misleading in some important ways, which I will mention shortly. The second is the translation by Werner S. Pluhar (Indianapolis: Hackett Publishing Company, 1996), which seeks to combine consistency in the translation of key terms with readability. Although it is largely effective in doing this, it is sometimes unidiomatic or choppy. The third, which tends to be favored in current scholarly work, is the translation by Paul Guyer and Allen W. Wood (Cambridge: Cambridge Press, 1998), which is consistent in the translation of key terms and also follows the German sentence structure as closely as possible. While this can be useful, it often produces awkward and ungainly English that is hard on readers who are not specialists.

In this book, quotations from the *Critique of Pure Reason* are taken from Kemp Smith's translation, but I omit material that

Kemp Smith has added in square brackets, and I systematically make two important changes which I will explain shortly. I make note of a few further adjustments where the applicable passages are quoted. As a result of these changes and adjustments, many of my quotations from the *Critique* do not match the corresponding passages in any of the abovementioned translations. This is, I believe, a good thing, because it will help expose those who read the *Critique* in parallel to this book—including students who are taking a text-based course on the *Critique*—to different attempts to render Kant's text in English. This can be a significant aid to understanding.

My first major systematic change to Kemp Smith's translation is to follow the other two translations in rendering *Erkenntnis* as *cognition* rather than as *knowledge*. In defense of Kemp Smith's rendition of *Erkenntnis*, it could be observed that in everyday German this word is sometimes equivalent to the English word *knowledge*—but it is often closer to *understanding*. In any case, *knowledge* is misleading in a way that *cognition* is not, because Kant often applies *Erkenntnis* to things other than knowledge. As noted in Chapter 2, these include judgments that do not express knowledge, concepts, and even aspects of intuitions (i.e., perceptual presentations). In some cases, Kemp Smith handles this problem by translating *Erkenntnis* into an English phrase that includes the word *knowledge*—for example, "modes of knowledge" (B3). A related grammatical problem is that Kant often uses *Erkenntnis* in the plural (see, for example, Avii and B3) and sometimes with the indefinite article (see, for example, B1). These forms work well enough with *cognition* but not with *knowledge*. Kemp Smith accordingly avoids both forms, sometimes by circumlocution (as in "modes of knowledge"—B3) and sometimes by replacing the indefinite article with another determiner (as in "that knowledge"—B1). In quotations in which any of the abovementioned problems strikes me as potentially significant, I make further minor adjustments to Kemp Smith's translations of phrases containing the word *Erkenntnis* (without signaling that I am doing this) so that these phrases are closer to the original.

My second major systematic change to Kemp Smith's translation is that I follow Pluhar in rendering *Vorstellung* as *presentation* rather than as *representation* (a much more common translation, which is also used by Guyer and Wood). I do this because the verbal root of the noun *Vorstellung* is *vorstellen*, which means *to present, put forward*, or *introduce*, but not (in the basic case) *to represent*; and because *presentation* captures the important fact that intuitions present—or "give"—objects to us rather than re-presenting them (as if they must have been presented previously in some other way). For the same reason, I also change Kemp Smith's translation of *vorstellen* from *represent* to *present*. I do recognize that there are considerations that favor translating *Vorstellung* as *representation*, including the fact that Kant sometimes adds the Latin *repraesentatio* in parenthesis after *Vorstellung*. But, to be candid, my preference for translating *Vorstellung* as *presentation* is in part motivated by the fear that the term *representation* may tempt some of those who are new to the *Critique* to assume that Kant is committed to a representational theory of perception—a danger I don't think it is possible to forestall merely by adding a cautionary note when the term is first introduced.

Citations of passages in works by Kant other than the *Critique of Pure Reason* are based on the volume of the authoritative *Akademie* edition of his works in which the cited work appears and the pagination of that volume. This pagination is often indicated in translations, usually in the margins. Quotations from these works are taken from the following translations, but in all quotations I change the rendition of *vorstellen* and its cognates to the appropriate cognate of the English verb *to present* for the sake of consistency with quotations from the *Critique of Pure Reason*.

Anthropology From a Pragmatic Point of View (1798): edited and translated by Robert B. Louden (Cambridge: Cambridge University Press, 2006).

Critique of Practical Reason (1788): edited and translated by Werner S. Pluhar (Indianapolis: Hackett Publishing Company, 2002).

Critique of Judgment (1790): edited and translated by Werner S. Pluhar—and accompanied by a translation of Kant's unpublished first introduction to the *Critique of Judgment* (Indianapolis: Hackett Publishing Company, 1987).

Grounding for the Metaphysics of Morals (1785): translated by James W. Ellington (Indianapolis: Hackett Publishing Company, 1981).

Jäsche Logic (1800) (an edited version of Kant's lecture notes
   prepared and published by Gottlob Benjamin Jäsche with
   Kant's approval): in Immanuel Kant, *Lectures on Logic*, edited
   and translated by J. Michael Young (Cambridge: Cambridge
   University Press, 1992): 517–640.

New Elucidation of the First Principles of Metaphysical Cognition
   (1755): in Immanuel Kant, *Theoretical Philosophy, 1755-1770*,
   translated and edited by David Walford in collaboration with
   Ralf Meerbote (Cambridge: Cambridge University Press, 1992):
   1–46.

Notes and Fragments (published posthumously), edited by Paul
   Guyer and translated by Curtis Bowman, Paul Guyer and
   Frederick Rauscher (Cambridge:, Cambridge University Press,
   2005).

*Prolegomena to Any Future Metaphysics that Will Be
   Able to Come Forward as Science* (1783) (abbreviated
   as "*Prolegomena*"): translation by James W. Ellington
   (Indianapolis: Hackett Publishing Company, 2001).

1

Background

The aim of philosophy, abstractly formulated, is to understand how things in the broadest possible sense of the term hang together in the broadest possible sense of the term.
—WILFRID SELLARS[1]

1.1 The Basic Structure of Our World

The world that we human beings experience has certain broad, general, and very abstract features that deserve our attention. Let us review these *basic structural features of our world*, as we may call them.

Our world, to begin with, consists of *things*—such as stars, islands, rocks, trees, fruits, animals, human beings, tables, and computers—and stuffs—such as water, wine, gold, dirt, carbon dioxide, and plasma. These things and stuffs *exist in space and time*. More specifically, they exist in *one* space and *one* time which together make up a unitary spatio-temporal system. And they are all spatially and temporally *extended*, which is to say that they occupy quantities of space and time (however small) and are neither point-form nor instantaneous.

The things and stuffs in the world *have properties*—such as being green, round, cold, metallic, heavy, aerodynamic, or mammalian—including properties that vary in degree or intensity. And they *stand in relations* to each other. For instance: one thing or quantity of stuff can be bigger than, heavier than, next to, inside, or above another; one thing can be between or not between two or more others;

several animals can be members of the same herd; one animal can be the mother of another; and one person can hate, love, or be in love with another. Things and stuffs in the world are also ongoing *substances* in which events and processes occur. So they *are subject to change and can persist through it*—as a tree continues to exist when it loses its leaves, or you continue to exist when you fall in love or your hair turns grey. But they may not exist forever. They can *come to be*, arising out of what was previously there—as a tree grows from a fertilized seed and the nutrients that it absorbs and processes. And they can *cease to be*, turning into something else—as a building becomes a pile of rubble or an animal becomes a corpse.

The events and processes that occur in the world are *caused*, which is to say that something makes them happen. Indeed, they are part of *a single, pervasively interconnected causal system*. Even events in remote galaxies are or could be causally connected with things that happen here and now. That's how we can know about them. In contrast, fictional events—such as the events in a Harry Potter story—cannot be connected in this way with the here and now. This is part of what makes them fictional. But it goes without saying that the writing and reading of a work of fiction are processes within the real world's causal system.

We may well wonder whether it's just a brute fact that our world has such structural features, or whether they can be explained. Perhaps the most obvious response to this question is that most or all of the basic structural features of our world are just brute facts that cannot be explained. Someone who takes this line could well say, "That's just the way things are; they might have been different, but they're not." It is reasonable to think that fairly straightforward realists such as John Locke (1632–1704) and Thomas Reid (1710–96) would adopt something like this position, and that they would add that we discover most or all of what we know about the basic structure of the world by means of empirical evidence.[2]

Another possible response is skeptical, claiming that some of what I have called the basic structural features of our world are merely ways in which the world appears to us, and that these appearances do not reflect reality. Gottfried Wilhelm Leibniz (1646–1716) and David Hume (1711–76) would give something like this response with respect to some of these features.

Leibniz was a leading Rationalist (with a capital "R"): a philosopher who holds that the most significant knowledge is based entirely on reason rather than on sensory experience. And he thinks that reason can show that space, relations between distinct things, and causation between distinct things are not real but mere *phenomena bene fundata* (well-founded phenomena) that do not reflect the nature of the reality underlying them. Reality consists entirely of what he calls "monads": immaterial souls which have no parts and which cannot come to be or cease to be except by divine creation or annihilation. All real causation and change within the world, Leibniz holds, is internal to individual monads, whose properties are their continuously unfolding mental states. Everything else—including almost everything that we are ordinarily said to know about the world—is made true by facts about the monads. So, according to Leibniz, space, relations between distinct things, and causation between distinct things are not real.[3]

Hume was a leading Empiricist (with a capital "E"): a philosopher who holds that all our substantial knowledge about the world and things in it is based on sensory experience, as are all our legitimate concepts. Hume would accept that some of what I have called the basic structural features of our world—including its spatiality and temporality—are just brute facts that we discover through sensory experience. But, as he is often understood, Hume holds that we cannot know that things exist longer than our sensory impressions of them, and he thinks of ordinary ongoing things (or, as he calls them, "bodies") as mere projections of those impressions that cannot be justified. He also holds that we cannot know that all events and processes are caused, or that there are necessary connections between events that we regard as causes and effects. So Hume is a skeptic about substances and necessary connections.[4]

Leibniz and Hume were the two most significant philosophical predecessors of Immanuel Kant (1724–1804), author of the *Critique of Pure Reason*, which is widely recognized as one of the greatest works in the history of philosophy. Kant was a Rationalist in the Leibnizian tradition until he started working on the *Critique*; and it was Hume's skepticism about necessary connections which, Kant said, "first interrupted my dogmatic slumber and gave my investigations in the field of speculative philosophy a quite new direction" (*Prolegomena*, 4:260).* Kant's most thorough development of the core of this new direction occurs in the *Critique of Pure Reason*.

---

*For information about references to Kant's works, see "Note on Citations of and Quotations from Kant's Works," xv–xviii.

This brings us to a third possible response to our question about the basic structure of the world, namely, the response that is implicit in the *Critique* itself. Kant accepts that our world has the basic structural features which I have reviewed, and he regards most of them as necessary. These include, in particular, the spatiality and temporality of the world, the existence of substances and necessary connections, the causal dependence of all events on earlier events, and the pervasive causal interconnectedness of things in the world. According to Kant, it is no accident that our world has these features: it could not be otherwise given the way we are. For these features of our world depend, in a sense, on us—or, more specifically, on the nature of our cognitive capacities. This should not be understood as a pretentious expression of the facile claim that the way in which we experience the world depends upon our cognitive capacities. For Kant makes it clear that he thinks that the world which we experience—namely, nature—has these features. As I will explain it, Kant's view is that the world must have these features in order for us to be able to experience it. To make sense of this fascinating position, we must explore the *Critique of Pure Reason*. At this stage it is possible to provide only an inkling of what underlies it.

1.2 Knowledge and Reality

Kant's reasoning in the *Critique of Pure Reason* is to a significant extent driven by his interest in human knowledge and the cognitive capacities that make it possible. These capacities include, in particular, our faculty of perception, which he sometimes calls *sensibility*, and our faculty of understanding, which is our capacity to make judgments. On Leibniz's conception of knowledge, fully fledged knowledge of many ordinary things would require divine powers, but Kant is a humanist who is primarily interested in human knowledge. Although he sometimes mentions the idea of divine knowledge (or the knowledge of an infinite cognizer), he usually does so in order to emphasize certain features of human knowledge by way of contrast. And he is not a skeptic about human knowledge. Indeed, he accepts that human beings have objective knowledge and seeks to understand how this is possible. At the same time, Kant is aware that there are limits to human knowledge, and he draws on his account of how objective human knowledge is possible in order to identify and explain these limits.

Kant recognizes that most human knowledge of matters of fact is empirical knowledge—or, as he often calls it, *a posteriori* knowledge. Typical *a posteriori* knowledge depends in fairly straightforward ways on the evidence of perception. Most of our everyday knowledge about ordinary things in our environment depends upon our own observations of them and reports from others about their observations. And most of our scientific knowledge depends upon information obtained through observation. In the case of such everyday and scientific knowledge, perception provides evidential support for judgments that express the knowledge.

But perception can do this only if it is responsive to facts that make a difference to whether these judgments are true. It is important to recognize that this requirement is satisfied only if our perceptions might have counted *against* the judgments if the perceptions had been sufficiently different. For example, my perception of a cat sitting in an otherwise empty room provides evidential support for my judgment that there's at least one mammal other than me present only because I might have perceived a completely empty room, which would have counted against that judgment.

On the face of it, the judgments about the basic structural features of the world which Kant considers necessary cannot be supported by perceptual evidence in the same ways as the ordinary *a posteriori* knowledge mentioned earlier, because it is not clear that any possible perceptions could count against those judgments. Very briefly and roughly, the main reasons can be outlined as follows. It is not clear that any possible perceptions could count against the claim that the world is spatio-temporal, because all our possible perceptions present things as in space and time. It is not clear that any possible perceptions could count against the existence of substances and necessary connections, because this would require a lifetime of sensory states that are so chaotic that they could not provide a basis for applying the concepts of substance and necessary connection. (It is, indeed, arguable that such a chaotic stream of sensory states would not be perceptions that present things in the world, but—to adapt a phrase from William James (1842–1910)—just a "great blooming, buzzing confusion" of meaningless sensations.[5]) It is not clear that any possible perceptions could count against the judgment that every event has a cause, because failure to discover a cause of an event does not provide reason to think that there is no cause even if there have been extensive investigations. And it is not clear that any possible perceptions could count against the causal interconnectedness of things in the world, because perception itself is a causal relation, so anything perceived is causally connected to the perceiver and through the perceiver to other things. Or so it would appear.

All this is very sketchy, but it is enough to suggest that the claims about the basic structural features of the world which Kant considers necessary are not ordinary *a posteriori* judgments. As we will see, Kant thinks that they are not *a posteriori* at all, but *a priori*, which is to say that they are not empirical. But at this stage it is enough to notice that they do not express ordinary empirical knowledge.

Kant nevertheless holds that our ordinary *a posteriori* knowledge presupposes the truth of these judgments. And he explains this by treating these judgments as expressions of necessary conditions of the possibility of objective empirical judgments which arise from the nature of our cognitive capacities. To get a preliminary sense of the sort of thing he has in mind, notice that we cannot judge that anything that appears to us is objectively the case unless we implicitly take it to be part of a spatio-temporal world which contains substances and necessary connections, and in which all events are caused by earlier events and all things are interconnected. So the world to which our ordinary empirical knowledge applies— namely, nature—must have these features. The arguments in the *Critique of Pure Reason* that support this position are complex and challenging. The following chapters aim to make sense of the most important of these arguments and of Kant's account of their most important consequences.

1.3 The *Critique of Pure Reason*

Kant, who never married, spent almost his entire life in the East Prussian city of Königsberg, which is now the Russian city of Kaliningrad. He studied at the Albertina University of Königsberg and later went on to teach there, first as a private tutor and then as a lecturer. He covered a wide range of subjects, including philosophy, anthropology, jurisprudence, physical geography, physics, and mathematics. At the same time, he steadily published significant work in both philosophy and science, to which he made major contributions. For example, Kant's publications in physics included his *Universal Natural History and Theory of the Heavens* (1755), in which he developed one of the earliest versions of the nebular hypothesis, according to which galaxies arise from rotating nebulae, that is, clouds of gas. Pierre Laplace (1749–1827) subsequently advanced a more detailed version of the same hypothesis, which came to be known as the Kant–Laplace hypothesis. The current version of the nebular hypothesis is still the most widely accepted model of the formation of planetary systems.

In 1770, at the age of forty-six, Kant was appointed as professor of logic and metaphysics at the Albertina University and published his professorial *Inaugural Dissertation*. During the next ten years—his "silent decade"—he published very little because he was working on his groundbreaking masterpiece, the *Critique of Pure Reason*, which agrees with his *Inaugural Dissertation* on the source of our concepts of space and time but goes way beyond it on almost everything else.

The first edition of the *Critique* ("A") was published in 1781. This was followed by the *Prolegomena to Any Future Metaphysics that Will Be Able to Come Forward as Science* (1783), which Kant wrote to make the *Critique* more accessible, and the second edition of the *Critique* ("B") (1787), in which he revises many portions of the first edition and completely replaces others in order to improve his exposition. But he notes in the Preface to the second edition that "In the propositions themselves and their proofs, and also in the form and completeness of the plan" he has "found nothing to alter" (Bxxxvii). After 1781 Kant also published numerous other works which extended the reach of the critical philosophy introduced by the *Critique of Pure Reason*. These include, most notably, the *Grounding for the Metaphysics of Morals* (1785), the *Metaphysical Foundations of Natural Science* (1786), the *Critique of Practical Reason* (1788), the *Critique of Judgment* (1790), and the *Metaphysics of Morals* (1797).

The *Critique of Pure Reason* has had, and continues to have, an enormous impact on Western philosophy. It very soon attracted widespread attention in Germany, where it ended the reign of Rationalism and stimulated the development of absolute idealism, which is committed to an identity of thought and being.[6] It has also been widely influential within other philosophical traditions, including phenomenology and analytical philosophy. Today the *Critique* is studied and cited not only by Kant scholars and historians of ideas but also by thinkers grappling with live philosophical issues who consider it a rich and enduring source of inspiration, challenges, and ideas.

The *Critique of Pure Reason* is a very long book that takes up almost 900 pages in the original version of the second edition. It is also a very difficult book that is often unclear. One reason for this is that Kant was not, on the whole, an eloquent writer (although he does have moments of eloquence from time to time). Another reason for the difficulty of the *Critique* is that the views which Kant advances in it were so revolutionary that he did not have access to ready-made terminology for expressing them. So he had to adapt, stretch, and often overwork the available vocabulary. As he observes at one point, "obscurities . . . are unavoidable in an enterprise never before attempted" (A98). In trying to come to grips with Kant's thinking in the *Critique*, scholars must delve deeply into both editions and Kant's other works, notes, and fragments. They must also address many different interpretations of Kant's views and arguments in the scholarly literature on the *Critique*, which is huge and is still growing rapidly.

This introduction to the *Critique of Pure Reason* concentrates on key portions of the second edition that cover Kant's most important claims and arguments and are essential to a basic understanding of his project. It also includes some supporting references to other useful passages in the *Critique* and, once in a while, in some of Kant's other works. I try to make Kant's thinking accessible to readers who are not steeped in philosophy even though this occasionally involves some oversimplification. I also try to provide a taste of Kant's writing by often letting him speak for himself through a carefully selected arrangement of quotations interpolated with explanatory comments. Whenever a section or chapter focuses on a particular portion of the second edition of the *Critique*, the applicable portion is specified in parentheses in the heading of that section or chapter.

I concentrate on matters that I take to be of ongoing philosophical interest and do not pursue matters of purely historical interest. And because, in Kemp Smith's words, "Kant crowds so much into each sentence,"[7] I often have to ignore things in passages that I quote or discuss. I also have to leave some loose ends untied. My overarching goal is, whenever possible, to interpret—or, to be candid, reconstruct—Kant's views and arguments in ways that make sense of them. My overall account of the *Critique of Pure Reason* emerges over the course of this book. I do not claim to offer the best or the most correct interpretation of the *Critique* but seek only to present an accessible and intelligible interpretation that can provide a useful starting point for further reading and reflection. Although I cannot avoid taking positions on questions that are disputed in the scholarly literature, I focus on the *Critique of Pure Reason* itself, and I discuss other scholarly work in the main text of the book only to the extent that this helps me to clarify the *Critique* and its philosophical insights. But I sometimes use endnotes to cite examples of works in English that advance various interpretations of claims and arguments in the *Critique*, including interpretations that are at odds with those I offer. I hope that some readers will go on to explore Kant's *Critique of Pure Reason* and the scholarly literature about it in much greater depth.

2

The Preface and the Introduction

Two Types of Metaphysics

2.1 A Science of Metaphysics? (Bvii–xxxi)

In the first paragraph of the Preface of the A edition of the *Critique of Pure Reason*, Kant expresses one of his most important claims:

> Human reason has this peculiar fate that in one species of its cognitions it is burdened by questions which, as prescribed by the very nature of reason itself, it is not able to ignore, but which, as transcending all its powers, it is also not able to answer. (Avii)

In this context, a "species of cognition" is a field of inquiry. Kant goes on to indicate that the field in which he claims that we cannot answer the questions which burden us—and in which we therefore cannot have knowledge—is metaphysics. More specifically, he is thinking of *transcendent metaphysics*, which is concerned with the ultimate nature of reality as it is in itself beyond the limits of all possible human experience.

Transcendent metaphysics deals with what Kant calls *things in themselves* (which he introduces on Bxxvii and mentions on numerous subsequent occasions in the *Critique*). He uses variations of this term to refer to objects that we could not possibly experience and objects insofar as they are beyond the reach of all possible human experience. Kant sometimes refers to things in themselves as *noumena* (or objects of the intellect), which stand in opposition to *phenomena* (or objects of sensibility) (see, for example, A254–6/ B310–12). But Kant also sometimes uses the term *noumena* much more narrowly for objects of a divine intellect.

It is not unusual for a book on the *Critique of Pure Reason* to include an early section in which the author advances his or her interpretation of Kant's position about the nature of things in themselves and their relationship to ordinary empirical objects. But this is a highly controversial issue that turns on the interpretation of many other things in the *Critique*. So I think we should avoid making any final commitments about it before it is necessary to do so. What is important at this stage is that, when Kant talks about things in themselves or things as they are in themselves, he is *not* concerned with ordinary things and aspects of things which we could perceive and think about, but which do not depend on our perception of or thought about them—such as objects in nature and their empirically accessible properties. He is concerned, rather, with things and aspects of things that transcend our powers of perception and cognition, and about which we could know nothing.

A good example of a question in transcendent metaphysics is the question of whether the ultimate constituents of reality are, as Leibniz claimed, monads. Kant holds that speculative questions concerning God, the soul, immortality, and freedom also belong to this field. So what he is claiming in the abovementioned passage is that although we cannot stop ourselves from asking questions about such things, we can never have knowledge of them. Sometimes he expresses this claim by saying that transcendent metaphysics cannot be a science.

Nevertheless, Kant endorses and tries to make sense of the possibility of a different type of scientific metaphysics. This metaphysics, which could be called the metaphysics of experience, concerns the fundamental nature of the world of our experience.[1] It incorporates an account of the basic structural features of that world (such as those discussed in Chapter 1), and it applies to all possible objects of experience but to nothing else. To contrast it with transcendent metaphysics, we may describe the metaphysics of experience as *immanent metaphysics*. This is in line with Kant's decision to "entitle the principles whose application is confined entirely within the limits of possible experience, *immanent*; and those . . . which profess to pass beyond these limits, *transcendent*" (A295–6/B353).

Kant begins the Preface in B with the very reasonable claim that we can determine whether a field of inquiry has achieved the status of science on the basis of its success:

> For if after elaborate preparations, frequently renewed, it is brought to a stop immediately it nears its goal; if often it is compelled to retrace its steps and strike into some new line of approach; or . . . if the various participants are unable to agree in any common plan of procedure, then we may rest assured that it is very far from having entered upon the secure path of a science, and is indeed a merely random groping. (Bvii)

Kant goes on to identify the fields which had, in his time, achieved the status of science as logic (Bviii–ix), mathematics (Bx–xii), and natural science (in the form of physics) (Bxii–xiv). But this did not apply to metaphysics, a "battle-ground" in which there had been no progress or lasting agreement (Bxiv–xv).

So Kant raises the question of whether metaphysics (broadly understood) could become a science. And he suggests that this is possible only if we reject the standard assumption that "all our cognition must conform to objects" (Bxvi). Given that metaphysics is supposed to be an *a priori* inquiry into necessary features of reality, that assumption cannot, Kant claims, accommodate the possibility of a scientific metaphysics. The reason is that it is only through experience that we can develop cognitions that conform to objects. Hence, under the assumption that "our cognition must conform to objects," a scientific metaphysics would have to be *a posteriori* rather than *a priori*. So it would not be metaphysics.

Kant therefore suggests that we may "have more success in the tasks of metaphysics, if we suppose that objects must conform to our cognition," an assumption that "would agree better with what is desired, namely, that it should be possible to have cognition of objects *a priori*" (Bxvi). This proposed shift in perspective is analogous to Copernicus's decision "to seek the observed movements, not in the heavenly bodies [which here refers to the stars rather than the planets], but in the spectator" (Bxxii, fn.). Kant claims that his "Copernican Hypothesis" (as it is often called) is successful inasmuch as it "promises to metaphysics, in its first part . . .[,] the secure path of a science," where the first part of metaphysics is "the part that is occupied with those concepts *a priori* to which the corresponding objects . . . can be given in experience" (Bxviii–xix). In other words, Kant is claiming that his Copernican Hypothesis makes sense of the possibility of a scientific metaphysics of experience. But he then goes on to assert that the reasoning that supports the possibility of a scientific "first part" of metaphysics yields "a consequence which is startling," namely, that in scientific metaphysics "we can never transcend the limits of possible experience" (Bxix). So the transcendent metaphysics of things that are beyond the reach of all possible experience—which would be the second part of metaphysics—cannot be a science.

In the Preface, Kant does little more than announce these conclusions, which he believes he establishes in the main body of the *Critique*. We will consider his reasoning in support of them over the course of this book. Here it is important to emphasize that Kant's assumption that "objects must conform to our cognition" should not be understood to imply that objects must conform to our cognition *in all respects*. Kant holds, rather, that insofar as we have or might have *a priori* knowledge of things (as in immanent metaphysics), the objects must conform to our cognition; but insofar as we have or might have *a posteriori* knowledge of things, our cognition must conform to the objects (see, for example, A92/ B124–5). Because Kant holds that we can have both *a priori* and *a posteriori* knowledge of ordinary empirical objects, we are going to have to take great care to distinguish between features of our cognition which these objects must conform to and features of our cognition which must conform to the objects. Not surprisingly, Kant describes the former features as *a priori* and the latter as *a posteriori*.

This raises the question of how we are to understand the term *cognition*, which has emerged as the preferred English translation of the German word *Erkenntnis* in recent Kant scholarship. In everyday German, *Erkenntnis* is sometimes equivalent to the English word *knowledge*, and it is rendered as *knowledge* in some translations of the *Critique*.[2] But *knowledge* is misleading in a way that *cognition* is not, because Kant often applies *Erkenntnis* to things other than knowledge, including judgments that do not express knowledge, constituents of judgments, namely, concepts, and even aspects of perceptual presentations (which he calls *intuitions*). This suggests that the term *cognition* applies to all knowledge and thought and their constituents. This very broad interpretation covers the ways in which the term is used in the material I have quoted so far—and plenty of other material in the *Critique*. But Kant sometimes applies the term much more strictly, as when he insists that one cannot cognize things in themselves (Bxxvi), one's soul (Bxxviii) and freedom (Bxxviii), but can still think about them. In this strict usage, transcendent metaphysics is not a "species of cognition," even though Kant describes it in that way at the beginning of the Preface in A. Cognition in the strict sense includes knowledge, possible knowledge, and judgments that express knowledge and possible knowledge. Unfortunately, Kant seldom indicates explicitly when he is talking about strict cognition and when he is talking about cognition in the broader sense. But when it makes a difference, it is usually not difficult to figure out what he must have in mind.

Near the end of the Preface in B, Kant explains why he welcomes his conclusion that knowledge is not possible in transcendent metaphysics. His reason is that the impossibility of knowledge of things in themselves, which would belong to the realm of theoretical reason, makes them available for the use of practical reason (which concerns action), where he thinks they are needed to make sense of freedom and morality. For Kant holds that if strict cognition and theoretical knowledge of things in themselves were possible, then "freedom, and with it morality, would have to yield to the mechanism of nature" (Bxxix).

Chapters 3–7 of this book are devoted to Kant's constructive account of the metaphysics of experience, which falls within the domain of strict cognition. We will examine Kant's criticisms of transcendent metaphysics (and his attempt to make room for the possibility of freedom) in Chapter 8, the longest in the book because of the range of issues it covers. Chapter 9, a short final chapter, offers summary accounts of Kant's transcendental idealism and his talk of things in themselves, along with a brief assessment of his achievements in the *Critique of Pure Reason*.

2.2 *A Priori* Cognition (B1–10)

Kant begins the first paragraph of the Introduction in B as follows:

> There can be no doubt that all our cognition begins with experience. For how should our faculty of cognition be

awakened into action did not objects affecting our senses partly of themselves produce presentations,[3] partly arouse the activity of our understanding to compare these presentations, and . . . work up the raw material of the sensible impressions into a cognition of objects which is entitled experience? (B1)

Setting aside the puzzling relative clause "which is entitled experience" tacked on at the end of this passage, what Kant is saying here is that strict cognition does not occur before objects stimulate our senses, which in turn trigger our understanding into activity that results in cognition. This view is straightforward and makes good sense.

The relative clause "which is entitled experience" at the end of the passage is mainly a signal that Kant uses the word translated as *experience* (*Erfahrung*) in two different ways. Borrowing from the American philosopher Clarence Irving Lewis (1883–1964), we may call these *thin experience* and *thick experience*.[4] Thin experience consists of the sense impressions which are caused by objects and are involved in our perceptual presentations of objects, and which also provide the stimuli that "arouse the activity of our understanding." Thick experience consists of the judgment and knowledge about objects and possible objects of perception that is produced by our understanding. So the metaphysics of experience concerns thick experience. Whenever Kant talks about experience, it is worth asking whether he is thinking about thick or thin experience—and in some quotations I will insert the word *thick* or *thin* in square brackets to indicate which applies. Kant's key claim in the first paragraph of the Introduction is that all cognition, including thick experience, is stimulated and therefore preceded by thin experience.

In the second paragraph, Kant immediately proceeds as follows:

But though all our cognition begins with [thin] experience, that does not mean that it all arises out of [thin] experience. For it may well be that even our [thick] experiential cognition is made up of what we receive through impressions and of what our own faculty of cognition . . . supplies from itself. If our faculty of cognition makes any such addition, it may be that we are not in a position to distinguish it from the raw material, until with long practice of attention we have become skilled in separating it. (B1–2, translation of *Erfahrungserkenntnis* changed from *empirical knowledge* to *experiential cognition*)

Kant applies the term *a priori cognitions* to cognitions that are "absolutely independent of all [thin] experience"; and he contrasts them with "empirical cognitions, which are cognitions possible only *a posteriori*, that is, through [thin] experience" (B2–3).

A priori propositions can, however, have *a posteriori* constituents:

> *A priori* cognitions are entitled pure when there is no admixture of anything empirical. Thus, for instance, the proposition "every alteration has its cause," while an *a priori* proposition, is not a pure proposition, because alteration is a concept which can be derived only from experience. (B3)

At this point Kant does not say why he thinks that the proposition as a whole is *a priori* even though this is more important to him than the fact it contains an *a posteriori* concept. But the above passage does make it clear that Kant applies the distinction between the *a priori* and the *a posteriori* not only to propositional knowledge and judgments but also to lesser cognitions, including concepts.

Kant begins section II of the Introduction by offering two criteria of whether a proposition or judgment is *a priori*: necessity and strict universality (B3)—where *strict universality* means that "no exception is allowed as possible" (B4). These criteria make sense because a judgment cannot be established as necessary or strictly universal merely on the strength of empirical considerations, which can at most provide evidence that a judgment expresses what is actually the case or that there are no actual exceptions to it.

On the basis of these criteria, Kant claims that (among others) "any of the propositions of mathematics" and "the proposition 'every alteration must have a cause'" are *a priori* (B4–5). These examples are plausible. The truths of pure mathematics are necessary, apply without exception to everything possible, and are established by the method of proof, not on the basis of empirical evidence. The claim that every alteration must have a cause is one which we implicitly treat as necessary and strictly universal insofar as we would not admit the possibility of an uncaused alteration even if we could not discover anything that caused it. And, as suggested in Chapter 1, not even the proposition that every alteration *does* have a cause has been established empirically, because we have not identified causes of numerous alterations which we have encountered.

The above two criteria of the *a priori* apply to whole judgments but not to lesser cognitions such as concepts. Kant offers another test of *a priori* concepts: if from an empirical concept we subtract all empirical material, any remainder is *a priori*. He presents this principle with the help of arguments concerning two examples. The first, which is meant to show that the concept of space is *a priori*, anticipates a more careful argument which we will consider in Chapter 3. The second, which is more plausible at this stage, is an argument that supports the claim that the concept of substance is *a priori* on the ground that "if we remove from our empirical concept of any object . . . all properties which experience has taught us, we yet cannot take away that property through which the object is thought as substance or as inhering in a substance" (B6).

2.3 The Analytic/Synthetic Distinction (B10–12)

Judgments of metaphysics—whether immanent or transcendent—must be *a priori* because they make claims that are meant to be necessary. But they are not trivial and uninformative, like the claim that triangles have three sides, or that grandmothers are mothers. In section IV of the Introduction, Kant introduces the distinction between analytic and synthetic judgments to differentiate between judgments that are trivial and those that are not. It must be emphasized that this distinction applies only to judgments, never to lesser cognitions. Indeed, the distinction applies most directly to *true* judgments and things that involve true judgments, such as knowledge, because (as we will see) all analytic judgments are true.

Kant defines a subject-predicate judgment as analytic if "the predicate B belongs to the subject A, as something which is (covertly) contained in this concept A" and synthetic if the predicate "lies outside" the subject (A6/B10). To illustrate these definitions, he claims that the proposition "All bodies are extended [= occupy space]" is analytic because the concept *body* covertly contains the concept *extended*, so one cannot think of anything as a body without implicitly thinking of it as extended; while the proposition

"All bodies are heavy [= have weight]" is synthetic because the concept *heavy* is not included (either overtly or covertly) in the concept *body*, so one can think of something as a body without implicitly thinking of it as being heavy (A7/B11).

In the Introduction Kant does not generalize this account of the analytic/synthetic distinction to judgments of all possible forms. He makes good on this much later in the *Critique* and also in the *Prolegomena* (see 4:267), indicating that an analytic judgment is one whose truth depends only on the principle of contradiction. As he expresses this point in the *Critique*, "*if the judgment is analytic,* . . . its truth can always be adequately cognized in accordance with the principle of contradiction" (A151/B190). The principle of contradiction is a basic logical law which says that any contradiction is false. So Kant is suggesting that an analytic judgment is one whose negation is contradictory. *All bodies are extended,* for example, is analytic because its negation, *Not all bodies are extended,* is contradictory. The contradiction arises because the concept of a body is equivalent to the concept of an extended object. So *Not all bodies are extended* is equivalent to *Not all extended objects are extended,* which is overtly contradictory.

As I have unpacked it, the idea that analytic judgments are judgments whose negations are contradictory suggests that analytic judgments are conceptual truths—that is, judgments which can be established as true entirely on the basis of conceptual analysis—and that contradictory judgments are conceptual falsehoods. Furthermore, Kant clearly holds that synthetic judgments are neither analytic nor contradictory. From these considerations it is evident that the negation of a synthetic judgment must also be synthetic; that some synthetic judgments are true while others are false; and that, if there are any judgments that are neither true nor false, then these judgments must be synthetic.

Understood in this way, the three-way distinction between analytic, synthetic, and contradictory judgments can be applied to judgments of all possible forms. It is easy to see, for example, that *Any person is either a parent or not a grandparent* is analytic (because the concept of a grandparent is equivalent to the concept of a parent's parent); that *Some men are not human* is contradictory (because the concept of a man includes the concept of being human); and that *Not all cats are black* is synthetic (because the concept of a cat does not include the concept of being black). But to keep things simple, let us now set aside contradictory judgments and focus on judgments that are either analytic or synthetic.

Because of the linguistic turn in twentieth-century analytical philosophy, the analytic/synthetic distinction is currently applied to statements rather than to judgments, and analytic statements are understood as what may be called semantic truths—that is, statements that are true in virtue of their meaning alone. But statements express judgments, and the meanings of words and phrases occurring in statements can be understood in terms of the concepts which they express (as when we say that the meaning of "grandmother" is *parent's mother*). So it can be useful to treat the conceptual account and the semantic account of the analytic/synthetic distinction as interchangeable. This move is not based on anything specific in the *Critique of Pure Reason*, which does not deal with semantics as such, but it is consistent with all of Kant's applications of the distinction that I will discuss.

Two further points are worth making before we consider Kant's most important applications of the *a priori/a posteriori* and analytic/synthetic distinctions in the introduction to the *Critique*. The first is that Kant scholars would undoubtedly want to refine and qualify my accounts of these distinctions. The second is that both distinctions were seriously challenged during the twentieth century, most notably by the American philosopher W. V. Quine (1908–2000).[5] Now, it must be recognized that there is plenty of room for further scholarly work on the proper interpretation of Kant's distinctions;[6] and also that Quine's attack on these distinctions casts doubt on whether they are sharp, apply clearly to all judgments and knowledge, or can be defined explicitly without circularity. Despite these concerns, the above accounts support particular applications of the distinctions that are clear enough to make sense of what Kant is up to in the introduction to the *Critique*.

2.4 Synthetic *a Priori* Judgments and Knowledge (B12–24)

Because Kant's distinction between *a priori* and *a posteriori* judgments is different from his distinction between analytic and synthetic judgments, it cannot be assumed that the two distinctions coincide in their application to judgments and knowledge. On the face of it, four combinations are conceivable, as displayed in Table 1. But are all four really possible? Kant quickly excludes combination 2 by noting that analytic judgments must be *a priori*. For, in the case of an analytic judgment, concepts provide "all the conditions required for my judgment," so sensory experience is irrelevant to the truth of the judgment (A7/B12). If the two distinctions pass muster, then the exclusion of combination 2 implies that combinations 1 and 4 are both possible. And it is easy to provide examples of each, such as *All grandmothers are mothers* in the case of combination 1 and *Not all cats are black* in the case of combination 4. But what about combination 3, the synthetic and the *a priori*?

Kant is totally committed to the possibility of synthetic *a priori* judgments and knowledge. In the Introduction, he supports this commitment mainly by means of examples, beginning in section IV with the principle of causation, "Everything which happens has its cause" (A9/B13). For reasons suggested earlier, he assumes that this is *a priori*. Here he seeks to show only that it is not analytic, but synthetic, on the ground that the concept of what happens (i.e., the concept of an event) does not include the concept of being caused. This is correct, as illustrated by the contrast between the principle of causation, which we could reexpress as *Every event has a cause*, and the trivial proposition *Every effect has a cause*. *Every effect has a cause* is analytic, because the concept of an effect is equivalent to the concept of a caused event. But *Every event has a cause* is synthetic, because the concept of an event does not include the concept of having a cause—so there is no contradiction in the concept of an uncaused event. As Kant recognizes, however, there is still an open question about what connects the concepts involved in synthetic *a priori* judgments, such as the principle of causation, because it "cannot be experience" (A9/B13).

TABLE 1 *Hypothetically Possible Types of Judgment*

	A priori	*A posteriori*
Analytic	1	2
Synthetic	3	4

In section V, Kant argues that in mathematics, natural science, and metaphysics "synthetic *a priori* judgments are contained as principles" (B14). With respect to metaphysics, he does little more than assert that in metaphysics we seek to "extend our *a priori* cognition" with "principles which add to the given concept something that was not contained in it," and on this basis he concludes that "metaphysics consists, at least *in intention*, entirely of *a priori* synthetic propositions" (B18). His discussions of mathematics and natural science are more interesting because of what he says about particular examples.

Kant takes it for granted that the truths of pure mathematics are "always . . . *a priori*" on the ground that "they carry with them necessity" (B14). But are they analytic or synthetic? Focusing on two examples, he argues that they are synthetic. In the case of arithmetic, he selects the proposition *7 + 5 = 12* and argues that it is synthetic on the ground that "the concept of the sum of 7 and 5 contains nothing save the union of two numbers into one" but not "what that single number may be which combines both" (B15). In the case of geometry, he selects the proposition that "the straight line between two points is the shortest" and argues that it is synthetic on the ground that "my concept of *straight* contains nothing of quantity, but only of quality" (B16). Kant has been challenged with respect to both arithmetic and geometry.[7]

It has been claimed that the truths of arithmetic are analytic on the grounds that every natural number other than 0 can be defined as the successor of the previous number in the series and that arithmetical functions, including addition, can also be defined in terms of the successor relation. If so, then 2 is analytically equivalent to 1 + 1, 3 is analytically equivalent to 2 + 1, etc.; and arithmetical truths such as *5 + 7 = 12* can be established by analysis. This criticism has merit. But, in Kant's defense, it could be questioned whether standard definitions of arithmetical functions (which are rather complex), or the supplementary assumptions which are needed to yield the correct results (including principles of mathematical induction), express mere conceptual truths.

With respect to geometry, Kant meant his claim that the truths of geometry are synthetic *a priori* to apply to the theorems of the only system of geometry extant at the time, namely, Euclidian geometry (in which the sum of the internal angles of a triangle is always 180 degrees). A major challenge to Kant's claim arises from the emergence of alternative geometries during the nineteenth century, followed by Einstein's development of the theory of relativity, according to which physical space satisfies Riemannian geometry (in which the sum of the internal angles of a triangle exceed 180 degrees) rather than Euclidian geometry. This suggests that a pure system of geometry merely defines a possible space and that the question of whether the system applies to physical space is empirical, not *a priori*. But this holds with respect to each system as a whole, and it does not imply that nothing within a system is synthetic *a priori*. Moreover, as Van Cleve notes, if within a geometrical system a line labeled "straight" that joins two points is not the shortest between them, then it cannot really be straight. So, given that the concept of straight does not include that of shortest, *The straight line between two points is the shortest* is synthetic *a priori*. The same no doubt applies to some other propositions of Euclidian geometry, including *Two straight lines cannot enclose a space*, even if it does not apply to all of them.[8]

Kant backs up his claim that natural science includes synthetic *a priori* knowledge with two examples from Newtonian mechanics, namely, that "in all changes in the material world the quantity of matter remains unchanged" and that "in all communication of motion, action and reaction must always be equal" (B17). He assumes that these principles are necessary and *a priori* and argues that they are synthetic (B17–18). His assumption could be questioned on the ground that Newtonian mechanics has been superseded by Einstein's general theory of relativity, but it is understandable, and his argument that the principles are synthetic is compelling. In any case, Kant could have shored up his claim that natural science includes synthetic *a priori* knowledge by adding the principle of causation as a further example. This is also a good example of a principle of the metaphysics of experience.

Kant's most plausible examples help to support the claim that synthetic *a priori* knowledge is possible, but they do not explain how it is possible. In section VI, Kant sets the scene for the main body of the *Critique of Pure Reason* by identifying this question as "the proper problem of pure reason" (B19). Actually, the question that he mentions here is "How are *a priori* synthetic *judgments* possible?" (B19, italics changed). But he must be thinking of knowledge rather than mere judgment because it is clear that he is concerned with scientifically valid judgments, as in mathematics, natural science, and scientific metaphysics (see B20 and B22).

2.5 Transcendental Philosophy (B24–7)

In the last section of the Introduction, VII, Kant introduces "the idea of a special science which can be entitled the Critique of Pure Reason" (A11/B24) to deal with the abovementioned question and closely related matters. This field, he says, forms the core of what "might be entitled transcendental philosophy" (A12/B25), which is concerned with *a priori* cognition in general. The field is not meant to cover all *a priori* knowledge, but only to explain how synthetic *a priori* knowledge is possible, determine and explain its scope and limits, and present the most fundamental synthetic *a priori* knowledge. This is what Kant attempts to do in the remainder of the *Critique of Pure Reason*, devoting approximately the first 40 percent to his response to "the proper problem of pure reason." This is where he answers the question of how synthetic *a priori* knowledge is possible on the basis of his Copernican Hypothesis. (It is also where he presents his constructive account of the metaphysic of experience.)

To make sense of Kant's terminology, it is necessary to appreciate his very important but potentially misleading distinction between *the transcendent* and *the transcendental*. As indicated near the start of Section 2.2, what is transcendent concerns things and aspects of things which are beyond the reach of all possible experience. As indicated in the previous paragraph, what is transcendental concerns the possibility of *a priori* cognition (which Kant takes to be limited to the domain of possible experience). That is why the word *transcendental* occurs so often in headings and in names of important arguments in the *Critique of Pure Reason*. Unfortunately, Kant does not apply his terminology consistently, but sometimes uses *transcendental* when *transcendent* seems more appropriate (see, for example, A180/B223, A238/B298, A246/B303, and A478/B506). And he sometimes uses *transcendental* when both transcendent and transcendental factors are in play. In such cases it makes sense, in light of the above account of the subject matter of the *Critique*, to give special weight to the transcendental factors.

In interpreting the *Critique of Pure Reason*, it is really important to recognize that Kant is engaged in transcendental philosophy rather than metaphysics or epistemology as they are typically practiced today. This may be unpacked as follows. We must not understand Kant as merely arguing for a particular position on what types of things exist or are the case, how they depend upon one another, and how other things depend upon them, as in standard metaphysics. And we must not understand him as merely attempting to uncover what bridges the gap between mere belief and knowledge and to develop criteria of knowledge, as in standard epistemology. We must, rather, understand him as attempting to uncover the *a priori* cognitive conditions and the fundamental synthetic *a priori* principles which are presupposed by the possibility of our cognition and our knowledge of an objective world. As we will see, digging up the presuppositions of what we ordinarily take for granted is at the heart of Kant's transcendental thinking.

3

The Transcendental Aesthetic

Sensibility, Space, and Time

The main body of the *Critique of Pure Reason* is divided into the Transcendental Doctrine of Elements (B33–732), in which Kant develops and defends his substantive views in considerable detail, and the very much shorter Transcendental Doctrine of Method (B732–884), in which he discusses methodological and historical questions concerning pure reason without modifying what has gone before. We will concentrate on the Doctrine of Elements and will not discuss the Doctrine of Method in its own right (but we will occasionally refer to material in it). The Doctrine of Elements has two main parts: the Transcendental Aesthetic, which is the topic of this chapter, and the very much longer Transcendental Logic, which includes the topics of Chapters 4–8. The Transcendental Aesthetic is concerned with the basic contributions of our sensibility—that is, our faculty of perception—to *a priori* cognition. The title of this part of the *Critique* is explained by the fact that the word *aesthetic* comes from a Greek word for perception. But it turns out that most of the Aesthetic is concerned with space and time. The reason is that our perception is inescapably spatial and temporal.

3.1 Intuitions, Appearances, and the Forms of Sensibility (B33–7)

Kant begins §1[1] by introducing some important terminology and related claims. *Intuition*, which we would call perception, is what gives us cognitive access to objects. Kant's use of this term should not be confused with its use in contemporary analytical philosophy to refer to things that one is inclined to believe. An intuition, in Kant's terminology, is a perceptual presentation by means of which cognition refers to objects directly or "is in immediate relation to them" (A19/B33). Kant holds that "intuition takes place only in so far as the object is given to us"—which is "only possible . . . in so far as the mind is affected in a certain way"; and he goes on to inform us that "The effect of an object upon the faculty of presentation . . . is *sensation*" (A19–20/33–4). Concepts, in contrast to intuitions, are presentations of the understanding that do not give us objects but allow us to think about them. Kant insists that "all thought must . . . relate ultimately to intuitions, . . . because in no other way can an object can be given to us" (A19/B33).

This brings us to a potentially confusing Kantian term, the application of which is widely contested, namely, *appearance*. Kant introduces the term by saying that "The undetermined object of an empirical intuition is entitled *appearance*" (A20/B34). So an object presented by an intuition is an appearance, and appearances include empirical objects that are perceived. But Kant also applies the term *appearance* to empirical objects that are not perceived because they are never present to a perceiver, such as rocks on the unexplored floor of an ocean. And he applies it to empirical objects which we cannot perceive but can know about indirectly, such as magnetic fields. For he treats nature as "the sum of appearances" (see, for example, B163, B446 fn.), and he is well aware that not everything in nature is or could be perceived by us (see, for example, A226/B273, A493/B521). So an appearance is not an appearing, but an object that appears, an object that could appear, or an object for which there could be empirical evidence. We may assume that the empirical properties of appearances do not depend on either our intuitions or our other cognitions, because "our cognitions must conform to objects" (Bxvi) with respect to empirical properties. Our intuitions can present some (but not all) of these empirical properties directly, as a visual intuition might present a tomato as round and red.

One thing that I have not yet explained in Kant's statement that "The undetermined object of an empirical intuition is entitled *appearance*" (A20/B34) is the adjective "undetermined." What this indicates is that, insofar as the object is or could be presented by intuition, no concepts or other operations of the understanding are applied to it. But, to look ahead, cognizing appearances as existing empirical objects does involve such operations. Kant calls appearances that are cognized as existing "objects of experience"— which refers to thick rather than thin experience (see p.16). And, as we will see in Chapter 5, he holds that appearances get the status of objects of experience through the presentation of necessary connections between them. This leaves open the possibility that some appearances do not satisfy this condition, which Kant occasionally recognizes (see, for example, A89/B122, *Prolegomena* 4:290). We should, therefore, allow for appearances that are not existing empirical objects, and we may assume that these include, in particular, hallucinatory objects and objects in dreams. But it is important to notice that Kant holds that presentations of such objects are possible only because we have prior intuitions of existing empirical objects (see Section 6.5). Nevertheless, almost everything that Kant says about appearances applies to existing empirical objects that do not depend upon our intuitions; and we may assume that, in the standard case, these are the appearances he is talking about.

The above interpretation of the term *appearance* has been challenged on the ground that Kant often says that appearances are mere presentations (see, for example, A104, A369, A490–1/B518– 19, A492/B520). In line with this, he sometimes says things about appearances that apply to intuitions rather than to objects that they present (see, for example, A20/B34, in the paragraph immediately following the definition of *appearance* quoted earlier). This suggests that Kantian appearances are not independent objects but only presentations or mind-dependent objects of presentations.[2]

This subjectivist interpretation of Kantian appearances is very widely accepted. But in my judgment there are three good reasons to resist it. First, it cannot easily accommodate appearances that we do not or cannot perceive. Second, it is not clear how it can accommodate Kant's claim that (in the standard case) the sensations involved in an intuition are an effect of the object of the intuition, which implies that the object causes them. This claim expresses a crucially important commitment, for Kant insists that "Our mode of intuition is dependent on the existence of the object, and is therefore possible only if the subject's faculty of presentation is affected by that object" (B72). Some advocates of the subjectivist interpretation would respond that Kant holds that the object which causes the subject's sensations is not an appearance but a transcendent thing in itself. Against this, it is worth emphasizing that Kant holds that we cannot know of the existence of things in themselves, and that the only causation by things in themselves that Kant allows for in the *Critique of Pure Reason* is causation from freedom, which brings about actions, but not sensations (see Section 8.6). The third reason for resisting the subjectivist account of Kantian appearances is that it is not clear how this interpretation can accommodate Kant's view that in *a posteriori* cognition, "our cognition must conform to objects" (Bxvi) rather than the other way around. For, if appearances are mind-dependent presentations, then it is trivially true that they conform to those presentations, and so cannot be objects to which the presentations must conform.

I am therefore going to stick with the anti-subjectivist view that appearances of outer sense are, in the standard case, independent objects. This may be taken as emblematic of the anti-subjectivist approach to the interpretation of most aspects of the *Critique of Pure Reason* which I adopt in this book. The anti-subjectivist view of appearances does, however, raise the question of how can we explain the fact that Kant often describes appearances as presentations. The answer, I think, is that he does so in order to contrast them with things in themselves by emphasizing that they are objects of a kind that *can be presented* by intuition or are appropriately related to such objects. In fact, he sometimes makes this contrast explicit. At one point, for example, after calling appearances presentations, he goes on to say that although "appearances are not things in themselves," they are all that "can be given to us for cognition" (A190/B235). Kant's description of appearances as presentations may also have been influenced by a widespread tendency among philosophers in the seventeenth and eighteenth centuries to treat ideas (which are, in Kant's terms, presentations) as objects of perception or thought (as opposed to means of perception or thought).[3]

In order to explain his very original and surprising thought that sensibility makes an *a priori* contribution to cognition, Kant distinguishes between the form and the matter of intuitions. Generally speaking, things have a form only as instances of some salient type, and their form is what they have in common with other things and possible things of that type. In other words, their form is what is invariant between them. Their matter involves features with respect to which they differ, or might differ, from other things of that type. An intuition's matter, Kant tells us, is constituted by the sensations that it involves, which are, in the standard case, caused by its object. Its form is determined by the nature of our sensibility and provides, so to speak, the framework within which those "manifold" sensations can be "ordered in certain relations" (A20/B34). So the variable matter of intuitions, which is caused by objects, is *a posteriori*, while their invariant form, which is provided by the mind, is *a priori*.

Kant sometimes calls the form of intuition *pure* to emphasize that it contains "nothing that belongs to sensation" (A20/B34). He adds that "This pure form of sensibility may also itself be called *pure intuition*" (A20/B34–5). As this indicates, when Kant mentions pure (or *a priori*) intuition, he is, at least in the Aesthetic, talking about the form of intuition.[4] So his phraseology should not be taken to suggest that pure intuitions and empirical intuitions occur separately. All our everyday intuitions involve both *a priori* content, which is presented by their form, and *a posteriori* content, which is presented by their matter.

To illustrate these very abstract thoughts, Kant says this:

> [I]f I take away from the presentation of a body that which the understanding thinks in regard to it, [such as] substance, force, divisibility, etc. and likewise what belongs to sensation, [such as] impenetrability, hardness, colour, etc., something still remains over from this empirical intuition, namely, extension and figure. These belong to pure intuition, which . . . exists in the mind *a priori*, as a mere form of sensibility. (A20–1/B35)

In this context, "extension and figure" applies to the bare spatiality presented by the intuition rather than to the particular sizes, shapes and positions of whatever it presents, which presuppose spatiality. This is important, because differences between the sizes, shapes and positions of different spatial objects are obviously empirical.

In the first paragraph of §2, Kant distinguishes between outer sense, by means of which we perceive outer objects (including our own bodies), and inner sense, by means of which we perceive presentations in our own minds (which obviously depend upon us). Objects of outer sense are presented "all without exception in space," while "everything which belongs to inner determinations is . . . presented in relations of time" (A22–3/B37). So, at the end of §1, Kant says that he will argue "that there are two pure forms of sensible intuition, serving as principles of *a priori* cognition, namely, space and time" (A22/B36). It would be better to say that space and time *are presented by* the forms of intuition because, as we will see, the claim that they *are* the forms of intuition cannot be taken literally even if we assume that space and time depend entirely on the forms of intuition. We will consider later whether Kant is committed to this view.

At this point I would like to comment briefly on Kant's claim that "Time cannot be outwardly intuited, any more than space can be intuited as something in us" (A23/B37). This is puzzling because we perceive things happening outside us in both space and time. Kant apparently holds that time gets attached to intuitions of outer sense through intuitions of inner sense, but it would take a complex story to make good on this.[5] Perhaps he wants to avoid admitting two distinct kinds of intuition of time that might not be in complete alignment, namely, the form of inner sense and the temporal form of outer sense. But this risk could also be avoided by assuming that all sensibility has one and the same temporal form. So, in what follows, we may assume that Kant's phrase "the form of inner sense" covers the temporal form of all sensibility. This is consistent with his later remark that "all the relations of time allow of being expressed by outer intuition" (A33/B50).

3.2 The Presentation of Space (B37–41)

We now consider §2 and the first portion of §3, where Kant advances and supports his views about the presentation of space, arguing that "the original presentation of space is an *a priori* intuition, not a concept" (B40). It is not unusual for commentators to embed their remarks about these passages within a general discussion of the proper interpretation of Kant's account of the nature, or reality, of space—that is, his "transcendental realism" with respect to space.[6] But it is easier to make sense of the core of Kant's thinking in these passages if we begin by considering them in their own right, without regard to what follows them in the *Critique* (which we will get to soon enough).

The titles of both passages mention the *concept* of space despite the fact that they are intended to support Kant's conclusion that "the original presentation of space is an *a priori* intuition, *not a concept*" (B40, italics changed). This conclusion involves two claims. The first is that our original (or most fundamental) presentation of space is *a priori* rather than empirical. The second is that this presentation of space is intuitive rather than conceptual—or, equivalently, that our primary awareness of space is through perception (which is surely correct). Kant clearly holds that our concept of space depends upon the presentation of space in intuition.

§2 contains Kant's "Metaphysical Exposition" of the concept of space. A metaphysical exposition, Kant tells us, is a "clear . . . presentation of that which belongs to a concept . . . which exhibits the concept *as given a priori*" (A23/B38). The core of the Metaphysical Exposition of space consists of four numbered arguments in support of the claim that our original presentation of space is an *a priori* intuition. The first two of these arguments support the conclusion that this presentation of space is *a priori*; the last two support the conclusion that it is intuitive. The third argument also includes material about the claim that our most fundamental presentation of space is *a priori*, but I will consider this material later because it is handled more clearly in a passage in §3 that was added in the second edition of the *Critique*. What is most important in the four arguments of the Metaphysical Exposition can be expressed as follows. Here I will be brief because I believe that, all things considered, Kant makes a good case for his conclusion.

The first argument rests on the fact that all our empirical intuitions of outer sense present objects as outside ourselves, as having certain spatial properties (viz., their shapes) and as standing in spatial relations to each other (such as being above, below, or next to each other, or being between two others). As Kant expresses this point, "certain sensations"—namely, the sensations involved in such empirical intuitions—are "referred to something outside me" and to things "as outside and alongside one another, and accordingly as not only different but as in different places" (A23/B38). But the presentation of the spatial locations, properties, and relations of specific appearances by particular empirical intuitions of outer sense presupposes a general presentation of space. Because it is presupposed by all possible empirical intuitions of outer sense, this original presentation of space cannot depend upon the empirical contents of the intuitions, which arise from the sensations they involve. The original presentation of space is, therefore, *a priori*.

Kant expresses the core of his second argument as follows:

> We can never present to ourselves the absence of space, though we can quite well think it empty of objects. It must therefore be regarded as the condition of the possibility of appearances and not as a determination dependent on them. (A24/B38–9)

What Kant is driving at here is that if we abstract from everything that is presented in space by any particular outer intuition, we are left with a presentation of space. Because this is presupposed by empirical intuitions, it does not depend upon them. So, again, this original presentation of space is not *a posteriori* but *a priori*.

Setting aside the material that he presents more clearly in §3, Kant's third argument is meant to support the conclusion that our fundamental presentation of space is intuitive rather than conceptual. Kant divides this argument into two sub-arguments in support of the same conclusion. The first sub-argument is as follows. Our fundamental presentation of space is singular because "we can present to ourselves only one space" and "if we speak of diverse spaces, we mean thereby only parts of one and the same unique space" (A25/B39). Therefore, that presentation "is not a discursive, or as we say, general concept" (A24–5/B39). This argument depends upon the assumption that, while intuitions are singular presentations, concepts, are general and so apply to more than one thing. But although stereotypical concepts are general in this way, Kant himself makes room for singular concepts, including the concept *space*. So the first sub-argument is unimpressive. The second and far more important sub-argument depends upon the claim that diverse spaces "cannot precede the one all-embracing space, as being … constituents out of which it can be composed" (A25/B39). In other words, the parts of space depend upon the whole. This is significant because (although Kant does not make the following point explicitly) mere concepts of space and its parts, unlike the intuition of space and its parts, cannot exhibit the parts as depending upon the whole. For a concept of a space need not present it as contained in space as a whole, while an intuition of a space would do so. So our original presentation of space must be intuitive rather than conceptual.

The core claim of the fourth argument is that "no concept, as such, can be thought as containing an infinite number of presentations *within* itself" even if it "contains these [presentations] *under* itself" (B40). The very important difference between these relations of *within* and *under* may be illustrated by contrasting a visual intuition of a group of cats with the concept *cat*. An intuition of a group of cats contains within it intuitions of the individual cats that are seen in the group. But the concept *cat* (like the term *cat*) is discursive rather than intuitive, and it does not contain any presentations of individual cats within it even though all intuitions of individual cats fall under it. Now, our original presentation of space contains "an infinite number of presentations *within* itself," namely, presentations of all its parts—that is, the spaces in it. Hence, because no concept could contain presentations of all parts of space, our original presentation of space must be an intuition rather than a concept.

The first four paragraphs of §3, which constitute the "Transcendental Exposition of the Concept of Space," were added in the B edition. A transcendental exposition of a presentation is one that explains "the possibility of other *a priori* synthetic cognitions"— in this case the truths of geometry, "a science which determines the properties of space synthetically, and yet *a priori*" (B40).

In the Transcendental Exposition, Kant again argues that our original presentation of space is an *a priori* intuition—namely, the form of outer sense—this time on the ground that this must be assumed in order to explain how synthetic *a priori* knowledge is possible in geometry. Because Kant is thinking of Euclidean geometry, one might well wonder whether his reasoning is vitiated by the challenge to the view that the theorems of Euclidean geometry are synthetic *a priori*, which was mentioned in Section 2.4. I think not. For, as we saw in Section 2.4, some theorems of Euclidean geometry survive this challenge, including *The straight line between two points is the shortest* and *Two straight lines cannot enclose a space*. And there are other claims about space that Kant, not implausibly, considers synthetic *a priori*, such as the claim that "space has only three dimensions" (B41). We may, therefore, reconstrue the Transcendental Exposition as arguing that our original presentation of space is an *a priori* intuition because we could not otherwise explain the possibility of our having synthetic *a priori* knowledge *of space*—even if that knowledge does not cover all of Euclidean geometry.

The argument of the Transcendental Exposition (B40–1) can be summarized as follows. First, our original presentation of space must be an intuition rather than a concept to explain how this knowledge is synthetic, because "from a mere concept no propositions can be obtained which go beyond the concept." Second, this presentation of space must be pure, or *a priori*, because the applicable knowledge is necessary and so cannot be empirical. Third, this intuition can be *a priori* only "in so far as . . . [it] has its seat in the subject" as "the form of outer *sense* in general."

In light of what I have said about the Metaphysical Exposition, the second and third steps of this argument make sense. But the first step, as Kant states it, is too hasty, because he himself later insists on synthetic *a priori* knowledge that is not based on *a priori* intuition, including our knowledge of the principle of causation (the validation of which we will consider in Section 5.4). What Kant has in mind, however, is that synthetic *a priori* knowledge *about space*—as illustrated by the examples mentioned above—is based on intuition rather than on the analysis of concepts. This is much more reasonable than what he actually says. It is also supported by the procedure that was standard in geometrical proofs in Kant's time, namely, the construction of representative geometrical shapes that support a series of inferences guided by intuitions of the construction rather than by conceptual analysis. (Kant provides a useful example in the Doctrine of Method—see A716–17/B744–5.)

3.3 The Reality of Space (B42–5)

The portion of §3 that follows the Transcendental Exposition has the title "Conclusions from the above Concepts" (A26/B42). Here Kant advances his initial views about the reality of space on the basis of his thesis that our original presentation of space is an *a priori* intuition. This is where he introduces his transcendental idealism about space (but note that this is only a part of his more general doctrine of transcendental idealism, which I will discuss in Section 9.1). Kant opens the passage by stating two particular conclusions and then proceeds to discuss them.

Kant's first conclusion is that "Space does not present any property of things in themselves, nor does it present them in their relation to one another" (A26/B42). His point is that space *as presented by the form of our outer sense* applies to appearances and cannot be attributed to objects that transcend all possible experience. For this presentation includes features that ground synthetic *a priori* truths about space, and transcendent objects are definitely not required to "conform to our cognition" (Bxvi) with respect to these features. Because Kant did not endorse conceptions of space other than that of space as presented by our intuition, he did not recognize that his first conclusion is consistent with the possibility of transcendent objects that have properties that might in some abstract mathematical sense qualify as spatial even though they are not presented by our outer sense. But he would have to insist that we could never know whether there are any such objects.

Kant's second conclusion is that "Space is nothing but the form of all appearances of outer sense," and that "It is the subjective condition of sensibility, under which alone outer intuition is possible for us" (A26/B42). The first of these claims (in which *appearances* must mean *intuitions*) explicitly identifies space (in which outer objects are, we may assume, located) with the presentation of space by the form of outer sense, and the second presupposes this identification. It is, however, important to recognize that the presentation of space and the space that it presents must be different things, because they have different properties. The presentation of space is a mental—or inner—entity. So, by his own lights, Kant should deny that it is in space, that it has any spatial properties, and, in particular, that it has the properties of space which it presents, such as having three dimensions. Hence space cannot be the presentation of space. So when Kant claims that space is the form of outer sense, we should interpret him as meaning that space is what is presented by the form of outer sense.

The problem of identifying space itself with the form of outer sense is not widely recognized in the literature.[7] Notwithstanding this problem, Kant's frequently repeated claim that space is the form of outer sense may be taken to suggest that he is a subjectivist about space who holds that the reality of space depends entirely on the form of outer sense. This would be the case if, for example, space itself were understood as a mere projection of the form of outer sense.

The outstanding advantage of the subjectivist interpretation is that it makes it obvious why space must conform to our cognition of space.

But there are reasons to question this interpretation. First, it seems to be at odds with Kant's commitment to "the *reality*, that is, objectively validity, of space in respect of whatever can be presented to us outwardly as object," which he dubs "the *empirical reality* of space" (A27–8/B44). Second, in the introduction to the Transcendental Deduction (which we will discuss in Chapter 6), Kant alludes to his distinction between a cognition's conforming to an object and an object's conforming to a cognition by contrasting cases in which "the object alone must make the presentation possible" with cases in which "the presentation alone must make the object possible" (A92/B124–5). He then claims that "In the latter case, presentation in itself does not produce its object in so far as *existence* is concerned, . . . but is *a priori* determinant of the object, if it be the case that only through the presentation is it possible to *cognize* anything *as an object*" (A92/B124–5). And he goes on to state that this applies to both intuitions and concepts. Kant's insistence here that an *a priori* presentation "does not produce its object" is inconsistent with the subjectivist interpretation of his account of space. Third, Kant holds that our cognitions must conform to objects with respect to their empirical properties. These include their specific spatial properties, such as their sizes, shapes, and positions. These properties must, therefore, be in the objects as well as being realized in space. But it's not clear how this could be the case if the subjectivist interpretation of space were correct.

An alternative interpretation—or reconstruction—is necessary. The key to a suitable alternative is provided by two of Kant's claims: first, that the spatial form of outer sense "is the subjective condition of sensibility, under which alone outer intuition is possible for us" (A26/B42); and, second, that "presentation is *a priori* determinant of the object, if it be the case that only through the presentation is it possible to *cognize* anything *as an object*" (A92/B125). What these claims suggest is that nothing can be an object of outer sense unless it satisfies the form of outer sense, which requires that it be spatial. In other words, spatiality is a condition of the possibility of anything's being an object of our outer sense. If so, then all nonmental appearances, which are possible objects of outer sense, must be located in space and have spatial properties. But this does not imply that the existence of space and the object's being spatial depend entirely on the form of outer sense. According to this interpretation, the spatiality of our world is not necessary absolutely—which is implausible—but necessary only for it to be a world that we can experience.

Notice that none of this implies that in empirical intuition we perceive space as such, let alone the whole of space. We perceive things (and some of their spatial properties and relations) as in space, which is presented by the form of outer sense. But space as it exists in nature goes beyond what we perceive in any particular empirical intuition or even in all empirical intuitions. The significance of this will emerge in later chapters.

Here we turn instead to Kant's transcendental idealism about space, which he introduces by asserting "its *transcendental ideality*," according to which space "is nothing at all, immediately we withdraw . . . its limitation to possible experience, and so look upon it as something that underlies things in themselves" (A28/B44). Notice that there are two sides to this account. One is that space as we are acquainted with it does not apply to transcendent objects. The other is that spatiality is a condition of the possibility of all outer experience, which explains how certain synthetic *a priori* knowledge is possible with respect to objects of outer experience. It is this second aspect of the account that explains what makes Kant's "idealism" about space transcendental rather than merely transcendent.

3.4 The Presentation and Reality of Time (B46–58)

Although they are organized a little differently, Kant's main claims and arguments about the presentation and reality of time in §§4–6 are largely parallel to his claims and arguments about the presentation and reality of space in §§2–3. But in the case of time, the synthetic *a priori* knowledge that the Transcendental Exposition seeks to explain on the basis of the claim that our most fundamental presentation of time is the *a priori* form of inner sense is arithmetical knowledge. This is not very plausible, because the link between time and arithmetic is much more remote and tenuous than that between space and geometry, for anything whatever can be numbered regardless of whether it is in time.[8] This includes abstract, nontemporal things, such as sets.

In any event, because of the parallels between Kant's claims and arguments about the presentation and reality of space on the one hand and his claims and arguments about the presentation and reality of time on the other, it is not necessary to review the details of his treatment of time. Instead, we will consider the significance of one notable difference between the case of space and that of time, namely, that while none of our presentations occur in space (because they are mental entities), all of our presentations occur in time.

In §7, Kant discusses a common objection to his position on time which hinges on this fact. The objection is as follows. "Alterations are real" (which Kant accepts because it is "proved by change of our own presentations"); and "alterations are possible only in time"; so "time is . . . something real" (A36–7/B53). Kant's response is to "grant the whole argument" (A37/B53) but deny that its conclusion is inconsistent with his position. We may assume that he would also accept the closely related argument that, because all our presentations occur in time, time is not something that is merely presented but something real. So it is worth asking how far this argument is consistent with Kant's position. It is, in particular, worth asking whether the argument is consistent with a subjectivist interpretation of Kant's account of time, according to which time as object depends entirely on the form of inner sense for its existence, so that it is, as it were, a mere projection of the form of inner sense.

The argument is clearly consistent with Kant's claim that our original presentation of time is an *a priori* intuition, namely, the form of inner sense. For this claim concerns only the presentation of time, not time itself. The argument is also consistent with Kant's claim that time as presented by the form of our sensibility applies only to appearances and is not "a determination or order inhering in things [in] themselves" (A33/B49). For all of our presentations are themselves appearances inasmuch as they are all possible objects of inner presentations. So the argument does not imply that anything other than appearances is in time. But the argument does make a difference to the interpretation of Kant's claims that "Time is nothing but the form of inner sense" and that, as such, it "is the formal *a priori* condition of all appearances" (A33–4/B49–50). It makes a difference because the conclusion of the argument—namely, that time is not something that is merely presented, but something real—is inconsistent with the subjectivist interpretation of these claims.

The argument is, however, consistent with an alternative interpretation that is analogous to my preferred interpretation of Kant's parallel assertions about space. According to this interpretation, nothing can be an object of our sensibility unless it satisfies the temporal form of that sensibility, which requires that the object be in time. In other words, being in time is a condition of the possibility of anything's being an object of our sensibility. So all appearances whatever must be in time. But this does not imply that the existence of time and the temporality of appearances depend entirely on the temporal form of our sensibility.

I close this chapter with two observations. First, given Kant's commitment to treating space and time and their presentations in much the same way in the Aesthetic, the fact that all our presentations occur in time not only favors the anti-subjectivist interpretation of Kant's position on time but also provides indirect support for the anti-subjectivist interpretation of his position on space advanced in the previous section. Second, Kant's transcendental idealism about time, like his transcendental idealism about space, has two sides: first, that time (as we are acquainted with it) does not apply to transcendent objects; and, second, that temporality is a condition of the possibility of all experience that explains how certain synthetic *a priori* knowledge is possible with respect to objects of experience.

4

The Metaphysical Deduction

Judgments, Concepts, and Categories

The Transcendental Logic has two main divisions: the Transcendental Analytic, which we consider in Chapters 4–7, and the Transcendental Dialectic, which we consider in Chapter 8. The Analytic, in which Kant develops his positive account of synthetic *a priori* knowledge of nature, consists of two books, the Analytic of Concepts and the Analytic of Principles. In this chapter we focus on Chapter 1 of the Analytic of Concepts. This chapter of the *Critique* is often called "the Metaphysical Deduction" because Kant refers to it as such on B159, no doubt because its relationship with the Transcendental Deduction (the subsequent chapter of the *Critique*) is analogous to the relationship between the Metaphysical and Transcendental Expositions of the Aesthetic.

The Metaphysical Deduction is the place where Kant introduces his categories. Categories are fundamental *a priori* concepts (see A64/B89). This means that they are *a priori* concepts that cannot be derived from other *a priori* concepts. It is no surprise that Kant includes the concepts of *substance* and *cause* (understood as a necessary connection) among the categories. For, as suggested in Chapter 1, he shares Hume's skepticism about the empirical credentials of these concepts. And, as we saw in Section 2.2, he argues that if we subtract everything empirical from the concept of an object, we are left with the concept of a substance, which must, therefore, be *a priori*. Kant could, likewise, argue that if we subtract everything empirical from our everyday concept of a cause—including succession in time—we are left with the concept of a necessary connection, which must also be *a priori*. Because of their centrality in the *Critique*, we will devote much more attention to these two categories than to all the others. If Kant can make a reasonable case for his central claims about these two categories in the Transcendental Analytic, this undoubtedly qualifies as a major philosophical achievement.

4.1 Sensibility and Understanding (B74–6)

Before we turn to the Metaphysical Deduction itself, it is worth discussing the first two paragraphs of the preceding introduction to the Transcendental Logic. This very important passage is transitional: it is here that Kant first considers the relationship between sensibility (the faculty of intuition), which is the main topic of the Aesthetic, and understanding (the faculty of judgment), which is the main topic of the Analytic. In this passage, Kant distinguishes between sensibility and understanding and discusses their contributions to cognition. In this context, *cognition* means strict cognition (see pp.14–15) and refers to judgments that express knowledge or possible knowledge—which depends upon links between the judgments and intuitions.

Sensibility and understanding are, Kant claims, "two fundamental sources" of cognition (A50/B74). This implies that neither can be reduced to the other. It is through sensibility that "an object is *given* to us" and through understanding that "the object is *thought*" (A50/B74).The presentations of sensibility are intuitions, and the basic presentations of the understanding are concepts. Both intuitions and concepts, Kant tells us, "may be either pure or empirical"; and they are empirical when "they contain sensation" (A50/B74). This account of empirical presentations is appropriate with respect to intuitions but misleading with respect to concepts, because concepts as Kant understands them do not literally contain sensations. But we may assume that concepts are empirical if their application depends upon the empirical contents of intuitions. Kant reminds us that "Pure intuition . . . contains only the form under which something is intuited" and adds that a pure concept contains "only the form of the thought of an object in general" (A50–1/B74–5). As this suggests, Kant holds that fundamental pure concepts of the understanding—the categories—arise from the forms of thought, or judgment. So in the Metaphysical Deduction, he seeks to identify the categories on the basis of the forms of judgment.

Kant insists emphatically that both sensibility and understanding are required for cognition:

> Without sensibility no object would be given to us, without understanding no object would be thought. Thoughts without content are empty, intuitions without concepts are blind. . . . The understanding can intuit nothing, the senses can think nothing. Only through their union can cognition arise. (A51/B75–6)

He hastens to add that this "is no reason for confounding the contribution of either with that of the other," but is "a strong reason for carefully separating and distinguishing the one from the other" (A51–2/B75–6). Here Kant is at odds with both Rationalists, who tend to treat intuitions as confused concepts, and Empiricists, who tend to treat concepts as mere traces of intuitions (see his remarks on Leibniz and Locke on A270–1/B326–7).

Kant often refers to sensibility as "receptivity" and to understanding as "spontaneity." He thereby contrasts the relative passivity of sensibility, the mind's "power of receiving presentations in so far as it is in any wise affected [by objects]," with the activity of the understanding, "its power of producing presentations from itself" (A51/B75). He holds that the primary acts of the understanding are judgments. As we will see, these are subject to our self-conscious control and can be made or withheld in light of our assessment of evidence. To the best of our knowledge, the only animals that have understanding in this sense are human beings.

Notwithstanding Kant's insistence on the distinct functions of sensibility and understanding, it is sometimes claimed that he is committed to the view that intuitions involve concepts inasmuch as their contents are conceptual. This interpretation is advanced most prominently by John McDowell in *Mind and World*.[1] A number of passages that appear later in the *Critique* can be proffered in support of McDowell's interpretation. In subsequent sections and chapters I will consider some of the most important of these passages in the contexts in which they occur. In this section, all I would like to do is prepare the ground for what follows by making a few more preliminary comments about the relationship between sensibility and understanding.

Kant's famous remark that "intuitions without concepts are blind" (A51/B75), which appears in an earlier quotation, might be taken to support the view that intuitions involve concepts on the ground that it implies that intuitions without concepts cannot present anything, and so are not, after all, intuitions. McDowell hints at this thought by means of a rhetorical question: "Surely, one might think, something that is blind would have to be totally devoid of representational content?"[2] However, it makes more sense to assume that Kant is not using "blind" to suggest that intuitions without concepts cannot present anything, but as a metaphor to indicate that, in themselves, intuitions are not within our control, conscious, or intelligible. This interpretation is consistent with Kant's metaphorical use of the words *blind* and *blindly* at several other points in the *Critique* (including, for example, Bx, A74/B99, A228/B280). It is supported by the fact that, immediately after stating that "intuitions without concepts are blind," Kant goes on to indicate that "to *make* our intuitions intelligible," we "bring them under concepts" (A51/B75, italics added), which implies that the intuitions are distinct from those concepts. And it is not much later that he confirms this by insisting on "carefully separating and distinguishing the one from the other" (A52/B76).

Note also that Kant makes it clear that he is committed to a firm distinction between intuitions and concepts in later work. For instance, his account of beauty in the *Critique of Judgment* (1790) presupposes intuitions that do not involve concepts (see, for example, 5:215–16 and 229–30); and in his first introduction to the *Critique of Judgment* (an introduction which he did not publish), he explicitly states that "intuition and judgment . . . differ in kind" (20:226, fn.). Ten years later, in the *Jäsche Logic* (1800), he says this:

> If we reflect on our cognition in regard to *the two essentially different basic faculties*, sensibility and understanding, then we come upon the distinction between intuitions and concepts. (9:35–6, italics added)

Because these works were prepared after the second edition of the *Critique* (1787), which Kant never repudiated, this information provides some (admittedly external) evidence that he was committed to a firm distinction between intuitions and concepts in the *Critique*.

It is important to recognize that the claim that human intuitions do not involve the application of concepts is consistent with the view that concepts can have an influence on the contents of intuitions. For instance, concepts that we take over from others can make us sensitive to different kinds of things and properties in our environment, thereby making a difference to what we perceive. But this does not require that these concepts occur within the intuitions themselves. It is also worth noting that McDowell moderates his *Mind and World* position on the relation between concepts and intuitions in a later work, where he claims that intuitions are connected with concepts only in the sense that "A potential for discursive activity [i.e., the application of concepts] is already there in an intuition's having content."[3] This, too, is consistent with the view that intuitions do not as such involve concepts.

Nevertheless—as we will see in Section 4.4, and in much greater detail in Chapters 6 and 7—Kant is firmly committed to an intimate relationship between intuitions and concepts, including categories. More specifically, I will claim that Kant holds that our sensibility and understanding are interdependent. On the one hand, all our thought depends upon perception—or, as Kant puts it, "must . . . relate ultimately to intuitions" (A19/B33). As this suggests, we could not even think metaphysical thoughts—or make analytic judgments—without being able to make judgments about sensible reality, which clearly depend upon perception. On the other hand, fully fledged human perception depends upon thinking, for we cannot perceive as normal mature humans do without ever exercising our capacity for thinking. As these observations suggest, we can deny that sensibility and understanding are completely independent without compromising the claim that they are distinct.

4.2 Concepts and Judgments (B91–4)

We turn now to the Metaphysical Deduction itself. Many commentators do not appreciate the full significance of this chapter of the *Critique*,[4] in which Kant aims to identify the categories by showing how "these concepts spring, pure and unmixed, from the understanding" and how they are "connected with each other according to one concept or idea" (A67/B92). He sets the scene in Section I, a discussion of the nature of the understanding that is brief, dense, and important.

The understanding, Kant reminds us, "cannot be a faculty of intuition" but is a power of cognition "by means of concepts" (A67–8/B92–3). A little later he adds that "the only use which the understanding can make of these concepts is to judge by means of them" (A68/B93). So concepts must be understood on the basis of their contributions and possible contributions to judgments. Judgments are "functions of unity among our presentations" (A69/B94). That is to say, judgments bring different presentations together into a unitary cognition. Consider the judgment *All bodies are divisible*. This combines the concept *body* and the concept *divisible* into a unitary cognition that expresses a commitment about objects. The unity of this judgment may be illustrated by contrasting it with the lack of unity displayed by a mere list of the concepts *body* and *divisible*, which does not express a commitment about anything. Although Kant does not say so at this point, a judgment is an act of *synthesis*, which he later defines as "the act of putting different presentations together, and of grasping what is manifold in them in one cognition" (A77/B103).

Judgments cannot present objects directly because only an intuition can be "in immediate relation to an object" (A68/B94), and judgments are composed of concepts, not intuitions. Kant therefore claims that "Judgment is . . . the mediate cognition of an object, that is, the presentation of a presentation of it" (A68/B93). He illustrates what he has in mind by observing that in the case of the judgment *All bodies are divisible*, "the concept of the divisible applies to . . . the concept of body, and this concept again to certain appearances" (A68–9/B93), namely, to objects presented by intuitions that fall under the concept of body. So concepts are "predicates of possible judgments" (A69/B94) which perform the function of "bringing various presentations under one common presentation" (A68/B93).

Two further features of concepts and judgments as Kant conceives them should be mentioned here even though he does not discuss them in the Metaphysical Deduction. The first, which is suggested by his characterization of concepts as "discursive" (A68/B93), is that concepts and judgments can be expressed in discourse, and hence in language. Kant does not say this explicitly in the *Critique of Pure Reason*, but he expresses the view that thought is closely tied to language in scattered remarks in various other works. (For example, in *Anthropology from a Pragmatic Point of View*, he says that "Thinking is speaking with oneself . . .; consequently it is also listening to oneself inwardly" (7:193).) The second feature of concepts which I have in mind—and this plays a pivotal role in the Transcendental Deduction—is that all judgments involve a form of self-consciousness which Kant calls *pure apperception*. This means that when one makes a judgment it is always possible to be conscious that one is making it. In Kant's description, it is "possible for the 'I think' to accompany" all one's judgments (B132). This is crucial to Kant's conception of judgment, for as we will see in Section 6.2, he regards the unity of judgment as inseparable from what he calls *the unity of apperception*—a unity that is related to the fact that different instances of the presentation *I think* that are produced by someone's apperception apply to "*one* self-consciousness" (B134, italics added).

4.3 Forms of Judgment and Categories (B95–101 and 106–13)

On the ground that "we can reduce all acts of the understanding to judgments," Kant claims near the end of Section I that "The functions of the understanding can . . . be discovered if we can give an exhaustive statement of the functions of unity in judgments" (A69/B94). He is thinking of the different kinds of unity involved in judgments of different forms. To illustrate, the unity involved in the judgments *All bodies are divisible* and *All emeralds are green* are the same because these judgments combine concepts in the same way. But this unity is different from the unity involved in the judgment *No snakes are indigenous to Ireland*, because this judgment combines concepts in a different way. In any case, Kant sees the categories as rooted in the forms of judgment, just as the concepts of space and time are rooted in the forms of intuition. So he would like a complete account of the forms of judgment— and the associated "functions of unity in judgments"—to use as a principled guide to the identification of the categories.

In §9 of the *Critique* (which coincides with Section II of the Metaphysical Deduction), Kant presents his account by means of his table of judgments (see A70/B95), which appears here as

TABLE 2 *Kant's Table of Judgments*

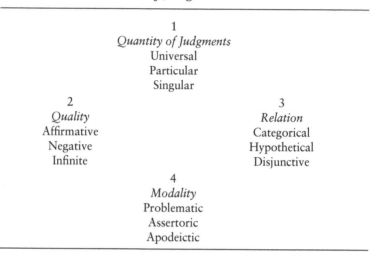

1
Quantity of Judgments
Universal
Particular
Singular

2		3
Quality		*Relation*
Affirmative		Categorical
Negative		Hypothetical
Infinite		Disjunctive

4
Modality
Problematic
Assertoric
Apodeictic

Table 2. The items in the table are meant to identify fundamental forms of judgment—or ways in which concepts can be combined in judgments—and the fundamental functions of unity in judgments which those forms express. Kant later tells us that we cannot give any explanation of "why we have just these and no other functions in judgment" (B146). The table depends upon the logic of Kant's time. Kant mistakenly identified this with the logic of Aristotle (385–23 BCE), which he took to be "closed and completed" (Bviii). But in fact Aristotelian logic did not deal with two of Kant's relational forms of judgment—the hypothetical and the disjunctive—and arguments that involve them. These were first explored later on, in Stoic logic, which was shaped largely by Chrysippus (*c.* 279–*c.* 206 BCE).

The forms of judgment included in Kant's table of judgments may be explained very roughly as follows. *Quantity*: a judgment is universal if it is about all things of a certain type; it is particular if it is about some unspecified things of a certain type; and it is singular if it is about a specified individual thing. *Quality*: a judgment is affirmative if it attributes a positive property; it is negative if it denies a positive property; and it is infinite if it attributes the complement of a positive property (e.g., *nonmortal*). *Relation*: A judgment is categorical if it unconditionally applies or denies a predicate to a subject, and thus expresses the relation "of the predicate to the subject"; it is hypothetical if it has an "if . . . then . . ." structure and expresses the relation "of the ground to its consequence"; and it is disjunctive if it has an "either . . . or . . ." structure and expresses the relation of a "divided cognition and of the members of the division, taken together, to each other" (A73/ B98). More specifically, disjunctive judgments, as Kant understands them, express "a relation of the parts of the sphere of a cognition, since the sphere of each part is a complement of the sphere of the others, yielding together the sum-total of the divided cognition" (A74/B99) or, as he put it later, "a whole divided into parts" (B112). *Modality*: a judgment is problematic if it makes a commitment to possibility; it is assertoric if it makes a commitment to actuality; and it is apodeictic if it makes a commitment to necessity.

To illustrate the application of the table with a few examples: *Necessarily all cats are mammals* is universal, affirmative, categorical, and apodeictic; *Some men are not beggars* is particular, negative, categorical, and assertoric; *Deuteronomy might not have broken it* is singular, negative, categorical, and problematic; *If Socrates is alive, then he is nonmortal* is singular, affirmative with respect to *alive* and infinite with respect to *nonmortal*, hypothetical, and assertoric; and *Any judgment must be categorical, hypothetical, or disjunctive* is universal, affirmative, disjunctive, and apodeictic.

I will not discuss Kant's defense of his table of judgments, because I believe that what is most important about his use of the table does not depend upon all the details in it.[5] But it is necessary to recognize that the fundamental forms of judgments include categorical form and hypothetical form—which is equivalent to saying that our faculty of understanding essentially involves irreducible capacities to make categorical and hypothetical judgments. This is important because of Kant's position on the sources of the centrally important categories of substance and cause, namely, that the category of substance arises from the categorical form, while the category of cause arises from the hypothetical form. It should also be noted that any shortcomings there may be in the table of judgments do not undermine the general idea of linking categories to fundamental logical forms of judgment and the unities that they express.

Let us now jump ahead to Kant's table of categories (A80/B106), which he presents in the second half of §10. (We will consider the first half of §10 in the following section.) A simplified version of the table of categories appears here as Table 3. In §11, a few pages after presenting his table, Kant says that the categories "may . . . be divided into two groups": those in classes 1 and 2 are "*mathematical*" categories, which are "concerned with objects of intuition"; and those in classes 3 and 4 are "*dynamical*" categories, which are concerned with "the existence of these objects" (B110). This suggests that the mathematical categories can apply to appearances regardless of whether they exist (or are objective), whereas dynamical categories can apply to appearances only if they exist (or are objective). Although the distinction between mathematical and dynamical categories is worth mentioning here, its full significance will become clear only in Chapter 5.

Given the supposed link between categories and forms of judgment, it should not be surprising that the table of categories has the same structure as the table of judgments. Before we assess the plausibility of the link, let us consider the claims of some of the concepts in the table to qualify as categories—that is, as fundamental *a priori* concepts.

As we have already seen, there is good reason to regard the concepts of substance and cause as *a priori*. The same can also be said about some other concepts in the table, as illustrated by the following two examples. First, the concept of necessity is *a priori* because empirical

TABLE 3 *Kant's Table of Categories*

1
Of Quantity
Unity
Plurality
Totality

2	3
Of Quality	*Of Relation*
Reality	Substance (and accident)
Negation	Cause (and effect)
Limitation	Community (or reciprocity)

4
Of Modality
Possibility
Existence
Necessity

intuitions cannot present things and properties as necessary. Second, the concept of negation is *a priori* because, while empirical intuitions can present particular things and properties and can also fail to present particular things and properties, they cannot present things and properties as *not* being present. For instance, someone can have an intuition of a tiger, not have an intuition of a tiger, or even have an intuition of a scene in which there is no tiger, but no one can have an intuition of the absence of a tiger as such. On the basis of particular intuitions, we can sometimes *infer* that something is not somewhere, but to do that, we must already possess the concept of negation.

I leave open the question of which of the other concepts in the table of categories are, as Kant claims, *a priori*. But even if we assume that they all are, we may wonder whether they are all *fundamental a priori* concepts on the ground that some of them may be definable in terms of others. Kant claims that in each class "the third category . . . arises from the combination of the second category with the first" (B110). He unpacks this as follows:

> Thus *allness* or *totality* is just plurality considered as unity; *limitation* is simply reality combined with negation; *community* is the causality of substances reciprocally determining one another; lastly *necessity* is just the existence which is given through possibility itself. (B111)

But Kant immediately goes on to deny that the third category "is merely a derivative . . . concept" on the ground that "the combination of the first and second concepts, in order that the third may be produced, requires a special act of the understanding, which is not identical with that which is exercised in the case of the first and the second" (B111). So the third category cannot be defined merely in terms of the first two.

Kant does not consider whether some of the categories in the table can be defined in terms of any of the others without regard to the four classes to which the categories belong. And somebody might well protest that *possibility* is definable in terms of *necessity* and *negation*, since the claim that something is possible is equivalent to the claim that it is not necessary that it is not the case. But I will not pursue such quibbles, because I believe that the details of Kant's table of categories (like the details of his table of judgments) are not crucially important to what is most insightful about his project. It is, however, essential that we recognize the concepts of substance and cause as categories. And there is good reason to regard some of the other concepts in the table of categories as *a priori*, including the concepts of negation, necessity, and possibility. In any case, I will typically refer to all the concepts in the table as categories even though I have left it open whether they can be firmly established as such.

Kant does not think that categories are innate concepts, so he owes us an alternative account of their *a priori* source. This is where the link between categories and forms of judgment comes into play. Kant holds that the categories are determined by the form of our understanding. Because understanding is the faculty of judgment, this suggests that the categories may be explained as conceptual expressions of the basic forms of judgment. The link seems obvious in the case of some of the categories in Kant's table, including *negation* and the categories of modality, which clearly fit the corresponding forms of judgments. In the case of some other categories, the link seems contrived. It is not at all obvious how, for example, *totality* can be explained as a conceptual expression of the form of singular judgments. Kant himself considers it necessary to explain the link between the category of *community* and the disjunctive form of judgments. His explanation is that disjunctive judgments include only those "either ... or ..." judgments that are exhaustive inasmuch as they present "a whole divided into parts," just as the category of community presents "a *whole* which is made up of *things*" which, unlike a cause and its effect, are "simultaneously and reciprocally ... coordinated" (B112). Despite the unclarity of the link between some categories and the corresponding forms of judgment, it is, as we will now see, reasonable to count the all-important categories of substance and cause as conceptual expressions of the categorical and hypothetical forms of judgment.

In Table 3 the category of substance is listed as *Substance (and accident)* to indicate that it is a relational category with two sides. In the full table it is listed as the category of "Inherence and Subsistence (*substantia et accidens*)" (A80/B106). So a substance is something which subsists and in which properties inhere. But this is, at bottom, the relationship that affirmative categorical judgments—namely, judgments of subject-predicate form—assert. The qualification "at bottom" is required because the subject of one categorical judgment can be the predicate of another. The concept *bodies*, for example, is the subject of *All bodies are divisible* but the predicate of *All rocks are bodies*. So it cannot be that anything to which a subject applies is a substance and that anything to which a predicate applies is a property. But we could say that anything to which a subject applies is a substance and that anything to which only a predicate can apply is a property. This is enough to count the category of substance as a conceptual expression of the subject-predicate form.

In Table 3 the category of cause is listed as *Cause (and effect)* to indicate that it, too, is a relational category with two sides. In the full table it is listed as the category of "Causality and Dependence (cause and effect)" (A80/B106). So the category of cause expresses a dependence relation. But that is what hypothetical judgments assert. So it makes sense to count the category of cause as a conceptual expression of the hypothetical form of judgment.

These links between the categories of substance and cause and the corresponding forms of judgment make especially good sense if one thinks of categories in their pure form, that is, in abstraction from all the empirical content involved in their everyday applications, including temporal factors. As this indicates, it is necessary to recognize a distinction between a "pure category" (see, for example, A242–4/B300–2) and what I will call a *natural category*, which incorporates this empirical content. In the case of *substance*, the pure category could be glossed as *subject of properties*, while the natural category also includes a criterion of the concept's application, namely, that it applies to things that are *permanent in time*. In the case of *cause*, a judgment involving the pure category with the form *x is a cause of y* is equivalent to the claim that *y depends upon x* (without further qualification). The natural category also includes the criterion that *y follows x in time as part of a regular pattern of natural law*. Kant explains the need for such criteria in the Schematism, where he notes that, without them, the categories still have a meaning "but it is purely logical" and "can find no object, and so can acquire no meaning which might yield a concept of some object" (A147/B186–7; see also A242–3/B300–1). Kant often calls such a criterion for the application of a category a *schema* (pl. *schemata*) (see, for example, A147/B186, A188/B231). But I will not follow this usage because, as we will see in Chapter 7, the term *schema* can also be applied to another important cognitive function.

4.4 Synthesis (B102–5)

The concept of synthesis is crucially important in the *Critique of Pure Reason*. We have already seen how Kant defines synthesis and why judgments involve synthesis (see p.48). We turn now to the first half of §10, a difficult but important passage in which Kant introduces the concept of synthesis and offers a general account of the relationship between the categories and the forms of judgment in terms of synthesis. Kant's reasoning in this passage turns on the thought that, if the manifold of intuition is to be made into a cognition, it must "be gone through in a certain way, taken up, and connected" by an act of synthesis (A77/B102). This holds for both empirical and *a priori* cognition. We begin with the case of empirical cognition, which is easier to grasp.

An empirical cognition in the strict sense is a judgment in which the key concepts are "applied . . . to certain appearances" (A68–9/ B93) by means of intuitions that fall under those concepts—because concepts cannot present objects directly. Consider the empirical judgment *Some cats are black*. What makes this a cognition in the strict sense is that the concept *cat* is applied to cats by means of the many intuitions that fall under this concept, and that the concept *black* is applied to black things by means of the many intuitions that fall under this concept. But what explains the fact that certain intuitions fall under a given concept?

It is important to recognize that the correct answer cannot be that these intuitions fall under the concept because they present objects (i.e., appearances) to which the concept already applies. The reason why this cannot be correct is that the applicability of a concept to objects is supposed to be mediated by—and hence to depend upon—the intuitions that fall under the concept. Kant's answer to the question is that "synthesis is that which gathers the elements for cognition [viz., the intuitions], and unites them to a certain content" (A77–8/B103), namely, the content in virtue of which they fall under the concept. To illustrate, certain intuitions fall under the concept *cat* only if all these intuitions have a common content that we could express by saying that they are all *cat-intuitions*, and this common content depends upon a synthesis that gathers them together and "unites them to . . . [that] content."

Here's a way to make sense of this (which we will explore more carefully in Section 7.2). A particular empirical intuition cannot have a certain content unless it is somehow associated with other similar intuitions that also have the *same* content. My current intuition of Muggle is a cat-intuition in part because it is associated with other relevantly similar intuitions that are also cat-intuitions, such as my intuitions of Jingly, Rupert, and Murgle. The contents of intuitions depend in part upon such associations or groupings, which are, in Kant's terms, syntheses.

Let us now consider the case of *a priori* cognitions, which involve pure or *a priori* syntheses. These are the syntheses on which the applications of the categories depend. In many places, Kant does not differentiate between different categories but talks about them in general as if they were one. This includes the first half of §10. The most important features of the relationship between pure synthesis and the categories which he identifies in this passage are that "Pure synthesis, *presented in its most general aspect*, gives us the pure concept of understanding," and that the categories are "The concepts which give *unity* to this pure synthesis" (A78–9/B104). So every category is associated with a pure synthesis on which its application depends and to which it gives unity. It is important to recognize that this implies that the category and the associated pure synthesis are distinct.

One of the most puzzling things Kant says about pure synthesis in the *Critique of Pure Reason* is that it applies to the manifold of *pure* intuition (see, for example, A77/B103 and A78–9/B104). But the all-important categories of substance and cause apply to empirical objects, not to empty manifolds of spaces and times. So how can the associated syntheses apply to such empty manifolds? I have not found an answer in the *Critique* that makes good sense to me. I therefore propose to adapt Kant's account of *a priori* intuitions as forms of intuition to the case of pure, or *a priori*, syntheses. On this approach, Kant's talk about *a priori* synthesis should be treated as equivalent to talk about the *a priori* forms of empirical syntheses—that is, general ways in which presentations can be combined that arise from the nature of our cognitive faculties. Kant considers the forms of synthesis associated with different categories in the Schematism, the topic of Chapter 7. So that is where we will consider the forms of synthesis corresponding to the categories of substance and cause.

Thinking about the synthesis of intuitions rather than the synthesis of concepts in a judgment, Kant claims that

> Synthesis . . . is the mere result of the power of imagination, a blind but indispensable function of the soul, without which we would have no cognition whatsoever, but of which we are scarcely ever conscious. (A78/B103)

He goes on to say that "To bring this synthesis *to concepts* is a function which belongs to the understanding" (A78/B103). Since synthesis goes beyond mere receptivity, this strongly suggests that Kant sees imagination as distinct from the passive sensations involved in sensibility as well as from the understanding. I will assume that he is committed to this view even though he sometimes seems to attribute operations of imagination to the understanding.

We come at last to Kant's general account of the link between categories and forms of judgment (or functions of unity in judgments):

> The same function which gives unity to the various presentations *in a judgment* also gives unity to the mere synthesis of various presentations *in an intuition*; and this unity, in its most general expression, we entitle the pure concept of the understanding. . . .
>
>   In this manner, there arise precisely the same number of pure concepts of the understanding which apply *a priori* to objects of intuition in general, as, in the preceding table [i.e., the table of judgments], there have been found to be logical functions in all possible judgments. (A79/B104–5)

Kant's general account of the link between categories and forms of judgment raises the question of why he holds that *the same* functions give unity to both the various presentations in judgments and the various presentations in the synthesis of intuitions. Given his view that the categories have their source in the forms of understanding, we may well wonder whether he thinks that the forms of imaginative synthesis underlying the application of the categories are sensitive to the forms of judgment in such a way that the imagination synthesizes the manifold of sensibility into intuitions that will fall under judgments.

We will consider the relationship between imaginative synthesis and judgment further in Sections 6.4, 7.2, and 7.3. At this point, one of the most important things to recognize is that Kant's claim in the Metaphysical Deduction that the contents of intuitions depend upon the synthesis of imagination is a significant addition to his treatment of intuition in the Aesthetic. It must be emphasized that this addition does not imply that intuitions directly involve categories or any other concepts. For the syntheses on which the contents of intuitions depend are not brought about by the application of concepts but by the imagination, that "blind but indispensable function of the soul . . . of which we are scarcely ever conscious" (A78/B103). Intuitions *fall under* categories because categories express the *unity* of applicable forms of imaginative synthesis, but this does not imply that the categories are directly involved in the intuitions or their synthesis.

5

The Analogies and the Postulates

Fundamental Principles about Substance, Causation, Community, and Modality

As mentioned earlier, the Transcendental Analytic consists of two books, the Analytic of Concepts and the Analytic of Principles. The Analytic of Concepts consists of two chapters, the Metaphysical Deduction, which we discussed in Chapter 4, and the Transcendental Deduction, which we will discuss later. The Analytic of Principles consists of three chapters, but we will concentrate on the first two, which are commonly known as the Schematism and the Principles.[1] The four chapters of the Analytic on which we focus in this book are the heart of the *Critique of Pure Reason*. The relationship between these chapters is, roughly, as follows:

1. The Metaphysical Deduction introduces the categories and gives an account of their source in the forms of judgment.

2. The Transcendental Deduction argues that we have a right to apply the categories to appearances presented by intuitions.

3. The Schematism attempts to show how it is possible for intuitions to fall under categories and thus how categories can apply to the appearances which those intuitions present.

4. The Principles aims to establish the fundamental synthetic *a priori* truths involved in the application of the categories to appearances.

We are going to consider some of the most important parts of the Principles in this chapter, postponing the Transcendental Deduction and the Schematism until Chapters 6 and 7. There are three good reasons to do this. First, it's easier to deal with the Principles at this stage because Kant's thinking in the Principles is less abstract and more accessible than his thinking in the Transcendental Deduction and the Schematism. Second, tackling the Principles earlier will help to prepare the ground for these more challenging chapters and make them easier to grasp. And, third, a discussion of some of Kant's most important fundamental principles will help to illustrate how much depends upon the Transcendental Deduction's claim to establish that the categories apply to appearances.

5.1 The System of Principles (B187–9, 193–203, and 207–8)

In the Principles chapter Kant seeks to advance a system of "Synthetic Principles of Pure Understanding" (A158/B197) consisting of principles that he regards as fundamental synthetic *a priori* truths. These principles are fundamental in the sense that "they are not themselves grounded in higher and more universal cognitions" (A148/B188). Given that they are fundamental, they cannot be established by deriving them from other more basic principles. But, as Kant notes, "this characteristic does not remove them beyond the sphere of proof" (A148–9/B188). He seeks to establish his fundamental *a priori* principles by showing that they express "conditions of the *possibility of experience* in general" (A158/B197). This is equivalent to saying that if these principles did not hold, then experience would not be possible. The experience referred to here—and throughout this chapter—is thick experience (see p.16), which includes objective empirical judgments.

Kant divides his fundamental principles into mathematical and dynamical principles, which correspond to the mathematical and dynamical categories (see p.52). Notwithstanding Kant's terminology, the mathematical principles do not include "the principles of mathematics" (i.e., the axioms and theorems of mathematics), but only "those . . . principles on which the possibility and *a priori* objective validity of mathematics are grounded" (A160/B199). I will not discuss the mathematical principles in detail because "They are derived solely from intuition" (A149/B188), and so do not go much beyond the claims of the Aesthetic. But I will give considerable attention to the dynamical principles, which are the main focus of this chapter.

The mathematical principles are the *Axioms of Intuition*, which correspond to the categories of quantity, and the *Anticipations of Perception*, which correspond to the categories of quality. Although one might expect three principles of each type, Kant provides just one overarching principle. In the case of the Axioms, this is the principle that "All intuitions are extensive magnitudes" (B202), which is to say that intuitions present objects (i.e., appearance) as occupying space or time. In the case of the Anticipations, it is that "In all appearances, the real that is an object of sensation has intensive magnitude, that is, a degree" (B207). The principle of the Axioms requires no explanation. The heart of Kant's explanation of the principle of the Anticipations is as follows. Perceptions of an object "are not pure, merely formal, intuitions," but "contain . . . sensation" (B207), which must have some degree greater than zero if it is to be there at all. But this non-zero degree of sensation cannot be an extensive magnitude because mere sensation does not present space or time. Kant concludes that the magnitude of sensation must be *intensive*. He adds that "Corresponding to this intensity of sensation, an *intensive magnitude*, that is, a degree of influence on the sense . . ., must be ascribed to all objects of perception" (A166/B208). Presented in this way, the overarching principles of the Axioms and the Anticipations can reasonably be understood as redescriptions of material covered by the Aesthetic.

But in his further discussion of the Axioms and the Anticipations, Kant makes it clear that he thinks they involve "synthesis of the productive imagination" (A163/B204; see also A165–6/B206 and B208), which goes beyond the Aesthetic. Kant's reason for invoking imaginative synthesis here is that he holds that all his fundamental synthetic *a priori* principles, including the Axioms and the Anticipations, concern the application of categories to appearances; and, as we have seen, this requires imaginative synthesis (see Section 4.4). But the role of imaginative synthesis in the Axioms and Anticipations is obscured by the fact that Kant does not record a separate principle for each of the categories of quantity and quality, but merely a single, overarching principle which does not involve specific categories. Be that as it may, further consideration of the relationship between the categories and *a priori* syntheses of the imagination must await Sections 6.4, 7.2, and 7.3.

The dynamical principles consist of the *Analogies of Experience*, which involve the relational categories, and the *Postulates of Empirical Thought in General*, which involve the categories of modality. These principles play a much more important part in the *Critique of Pure Reason* than the mathematical principles, and Kant explicitly states and defends a separate principle for each dynamical category. After reviewing the general idea behind the Analogies— which Kant describes as "transcendental laws of nature" (A216/ B263) and "laws of nature which are pure and completely *a priori*" (A184/B227)—I will discuss each of the three Analogies separately. I will then take a brief look at the Postulates, focusing on the Second Postulate, which concerns actuality. Finally, I close the chapter with some brief comments about the significance of Kant's fundamental principles with respect to the unity of nature and the ways in which Kant's claims about the unity of space and time in nature go beyond the Aesthetic.

5.2 Experience and Objectivity (B218–24)

As mentioned at the beginning of Section 5.1, Kant aims to establish his fundamental *a priori* principles by showing that they express "conditions of the *possibility of experience*" (A158/B197), where experience includes objective empirical judgments. This is especially relevant to Kant's Analogies, which he supports on the ground that they express basic necessary conditions of objectivity.

In discussing the Analogies, Kant tends to talk mainly about objective time rather than objectivity in general, and he supports the Analogies primarily on the ground that they are required in order to explain certain features of objective time. Yet his reasoning is significant not only with respect to objective time but also with respect to objective space, and to objective things, properties, and events, which must be in objective space and time. Kant's reasoning presupposes a distinction between subjective and objective time. The subjective time-order of things and events is the order in which we intuit them. If I see a cat at the top of a tree before I see a dog at the bottom, then in my subjective time the cat's being at the top precedes the dog's being at the bottom. But if the dog actually got to the bottom before the cat got to the top, then in objective time the dog's being at the bottom precedes the cat's being at the top.

Appearances that are not objective, such as objects of hallucinations, can also occur in subjective time-order in relation to other objects within the same hallucination, as well as in relation to objective appearances. For instance, if I have a hallucination of a Madonna-like figure jumping onto the table and starting to sing and dance, after which I hear an actual dog barking, then in my subjective time the Madonna figure's jumping onto the table precedes her starting to sing and dance, which precedes the dog's barking. But appearances that are not objective cannot be in objective time—even though, when someone hallucinates, the process of hallucinating must occur in objective time.

Kant's thinking also presupposes a distinction between subjective and objective space. The cat is above the dog in subjective space if I have an intuition of its being above the dog; it is above the dog in objective space if it actually is above the dog at the salient objective time. Appearances that are not objective, such as objects of hallucinations, can be in subjective space—as, in my hallucination, the Madonna figure is out there on the table—but not in objective space. We will, however, focus on time, which is at the forefront of Kant's reasoning in the Analogies.

To get an inkling of what Kant is up to in his defense of the Analogies, consider the standard case of things and events that we take to be objective, such as the dog's being at the bottom of the tree before the cat is at the top. We could, of course, perceive the dog's arriving at the bottom while the cat is scrambling up the tree just ahead of it, but I am thinking of the case in which we perceive the cat at the top before perceiving the dog at the bottom without perceiving their getting there. In such a case, as we have seen, the objective time-order could be different from the subjective time-order. How, then, do we identify the objective time-order? Not by perceiving it, because the time-order of the perceptions is subjective time-order. Kant makes this point by saying that "the *objective relation* of appearances that follow upon one another is not to be determined through mere perception" (B233–4). But in the case of our example, we can identify the objective time-order if we have access to enough additional information. We can do so by figuring out the main connections between the cat's being at the top of the tree, the dog's being at the bottom, and other things involved in their getting there, and using these connections to ascertain the objective time-order. As this suggests, objective time-order is not the accidental order in which we intuit things, but an order that is necessitated by connections between them, including indirect connections mediated by their connections with other things.

Let us now consider judgments of objective time-order, for example, *The dog was at the bottom of the tree before the cat was at the top.* Such a judgment belongs to thick experience and makes an objective commitment. This objective commitment is, in turn, a commitment to certain kinds of connections (both direct and indirect) between the appearances that are referred to by the judgment. Hence the presentation of such connections is a condition of the possibility of experience. Kant expresses this thought in his statement of the common principle of the three Analogies in the B edition by saying that "Experience is possible only through the presentation of a necessary connection of perceptions" (B218). The Analogies therefore express what Kant takes to be conditions of the possibility of experience. And these, he claimed earlier, "are likewise conditions of the *possibility of objects of experience*" (A158/B197). Since objects of experience are appearances that satisfy these conditions, the Analogies also express conditions for the objectivity of appearances.

This account of the Analogies as specifying conditions of the possibility of objectivity should not be confused with an epistemological account according to which the Analogies express criteria of objective knowledge in terms of which we cannot know that something is objective unless we know independently that the criteria are satisfied. Such an interpretation might be expressed by saying that Kant holds that we *perceive* the subjective time of things but can only *infer* their objective time from their subjective time on the basis of the principles expressed by the Analogies.[2] But, if this interpretation were correct, then we could not know the objective time of anything, because we do not have independent access to the conditions of connectivity expressed by the Analogies. This skeptical conclusion is, however, inconsistent with Kant's explicit commitments, so we should reject the epistemological account. Kant's approach is not epistemological, but *transcendental* (see Section 2.5), for it seeks to establish the Analogies as synthetic *a priori* principles by displaying them as expressing presuppositions of objective empirical judgments.

What differentiates the three Analogies from one another is that each of them is meant to identify a different type of connection that is involved in objective commitments. It will come as no surprise that each of these connections is expressed by a different relational category. Kant associates each Analogy with one of "The three modes of time," which he identifies as "*duration, succession, and co-existence*" (A177/B219). So, as we will see, each Analogy is advanced as an expression of a condition of the objectivity of the corresponding mode of time.

But let us for the moment return to what the Analogies have in common. Two points which Kant insists on in the second half of the introduction to the Analogies deserve special attention. One (which comes up in the last paragraph of the introduction) is that the Analogies apply only to empirical objects and not to things in themselves. As Kant puts it, "these analogies have signification and validity only as principles of the empirical, not the transcendental, employment of understanding" (A180/B223). (Note, however, that in this context "transcendental" must mean *transcendent*.) Kant goes on to say that in the Analogies "appearances . . . have to be subsumed, not simply under the categories, but under their schemata" (A181/B223). This serves to indicate that these principles involve natural categories, which include temporal determinations, rather than pure categories, which do not (see p.55). This point is important because, if human judgment can apply only to objects given by or suitably connected with intuition, as Kant holds, then it must be temporal, which in turn requires categories with temporal determinations.[3]

The other important point that Kant insists on is that the Analogies—in common with the other dynamical principles and in contrast with the mathematical principles—are not *constitutive principles* but *regulative principles*. He explains this as follows. An Analogy "does not tell us how mere perception . . . comes about," so "It is not a principle *constitutive* of the objects, that is, of the appearances" (A180/B222–3). It is concerned "only with the *existence* of ... appearances and their *relation* to one another in respect of their existence" (A178/B220). And any such principle is "only *regulative*" (A180/B222-3). We can make sense of this claim by understanding *existence* in this context as equivalent to *objectivity*. In this light, the Analogies are not principles about what constitutes appearances as given by intuition but about what makes appearances objective. The Analogies, therefore, serve as rules of objectivity. So it is reasonable to describe them as regulative principles.

It is now time to reveal that, as far as I can tell, Kant does not use the noun *objectivity* (or, more accurately, its German equivalent, *Objektivität*) in the *Critique*. The adjective *objective* and the adverb *objectively* are pervasive in the *Critique*, where they express the general idea of reference to an object or to objects (see, for example, A109 and A155/B194). But Kant's uses of these words sometimes do not express what we would count as the idea of objectivity. This applies in particular in the Aesthetic, where the phrases *objectively valid*, *objective validity*, and *objective reality* occur several times (see, for example, A28/B44, A34/B51, A36/B53 and A40/B57) and are used to claim that space and time apply to all objects of sensibility, namely, appearances. But this holds with respect to both appearances that exist (namely empirical objects) and appearances that do not exist (such as objects of hallucination). For, as we have now seen, the Aesthetic is not concerned with the objectivity of space and time. In the Analytic, however, the words *objective* and *objectively* typically express a commitment to *the existence* of the applicable objects, and this is indeed a commitment to objectivity as we understand it.

5.3 The First Analogy: Substance (B224-32)

In the B edition, the First Analogy states that "In all change of appearances substance is permanent; its quantum in nature is neither increased nor diminished" (B224). In this context, the word *substance* refers to what we could call *ultimate substance*, which is supposed to underlie everything in nature and to persist through all change—including the coming to be and ceasing to be of *individual substances*, such as particular animals, plants, rocks, and tables.

Inasmuch as it claims that the quantum of ultimate substance in nature never increases or decreases, the First Analogy in B in effect expresses the law of conservation of mass from physics. In the A edition, the First Analogy states that "All appearances contain the permanent (substance) as the object itself, and the transitory as its mere determination, that is, as a way in which the object exists" (A182). This seems to apply more directly to individual substances than to ultimate substance.

Kant clarifies the First Analogy at the beginning of the "Proof" of the Second Analogy in a paragraph added to the B edition in which he reviews the First Analogy in preparation for his discussion of the Second. The core of the paragraph is as follows:

> [O]therwise expressed the principle [i.e., the First Analogy] is that *all change (succession) of appearances is merely alteration.* Coming into being and passing away of substance are not alterations of it, since the concept of alteration presupposes one and the same subject as existing with two opposite determinations, and therefore as abiding. (B233)

What Kant is claiming here is that all objective variation— and therefore every objective happening or event—involves an alteration of something which persists through the alteration, namely, substance. In the case of accidental change, both an individual substance and ultimate substance persist, while in the case of an individual substance's coming to be or ceasing to be, ultimate substance persists. The First Analogy's status as a regulative principle can be brought out by formulating it as the rule that *a change in appearances should be counted as objective only if it can be understood as an alteration in an individual substance or in ultimate substance.*

The basic idea can be explained as follows. Philosophers since the time of ancient Greece have agreed that *nothing can arise from nothing, nothing revert to nothing* (a principle that Kant quotes in Latin on A186/B229). But, subjectively, something *can* arise from nothing or revert to nothing. In my example of a hallucination, the appearance of the Madonna figure singing and dancing on the table arises from nothing and reverts to nothing. This is, however, a compelling reason to deny that it is objective. So the principle that nothing can arise from or revert to nothing functions as a rule of objectivity, and this principle in turn presupposes that there is something permanent—namely, substance—that persists through all objective variation.

These thoughts may also be illustrated as follows. Suppose that one has a long stream of intuitions that involve continuous, massive, and arbitrary variations—as if a random series of momentary views of a huge variety of different things were arbitrarily combined into a sequence. Then none of the changes in the appearances presented could be understood as alterations in substance or substances, so none would qualify as objective. Pushing this thought to its hypothetical limit, if a being's entire sensory life were of such a character, it could surely never develop a sense of objectivity. To adapt some comments that Kant makes with respect to causation in the introduction to the Transcendental Deduction to the case of substance:

> Appearances might very well be so constituted that the under-standing should not find them to be in accordance with the conditions of its unity. Everything might be in such confusion that, for instance, in the series of appearances nothing presented itself which might yield a rule of synthesis and so answer to the concept of . . . [substance]. This concept would then be altogether empty, null, and meaningless. But since intuition stands in no need whatsoever of the functions of thought, appearances would nonetheless present objects to our intuition. (A90–1/B123)

If this were the case, then the appearances would not be objective. (It should, however, be emphasized that Kant is committed to denying the possibility that "Everything might be in such confusion that . . . in the series of appearances nothing presented itself which might yield a rule of synthesis" that correspond to any category. I take this up in Section 6.5.)

In light of these considerations, I think that Kant is onto something important in the First Analogy. But his central argument for the First Analogy is not convincing. He summarizes this argument in the first paragraph of the "Proof," which he added to the B edition. Although Kant does not say this explicitly, the argument concerns objective time and objective time determinations. The argument is as follows:

> [T]he time in which all change of appearances has to be thought, remains and does not change. For it is that in which . . . succession

or coexistence can alone be presented. Now time cannot by itself be perceived. Consequently there must be found in the objects of perception, that is, in the appearances, the substratum which presents time in general; and all change or coexistence must, in being apprehended, be perceived in this substratum, and through relation of the appearances to it. But the substratum of all that is real, that is, of all that belongs to the existence of things, is *substance*. . . . Consequently the permanent, in relation to which alone all time-relations of appearances can be determined, is substance. (B224–5)

So the core of Kant's argument seems to be that, because objective time cannot be perceived, we need to posit ultimate substance as a substratum that provides a unitary objective time frame relative to which specific time determinations apply. Although this is suggestive, it is not clear why the premise is supposed to support the conclusion. So the argument as it stands does not provide a compelling defense of the First Analogy, and this holds regardless of whether the principle is identified with the law of conservation of mass.

But Kant supplements his central argument with further considerations that help to back up the First Analogy, including the significance of the principle that nothing can arise from nothing or revert to nothing, which we have already discussed. Kant also presents a more specific application of this principle in the form of an example:

A philosopher, on being asked how much smoke weighs, made reply: "Subtract from the weight of the wood burnt the weight of the ashes which are left over, and you have the weight of the smoke." He thus presupposed as undeniable that even in fire the matter (substance) does not vanish, but only suffers an alteration of form. (A185/B228)

This helps to support the claim that some empirical reasoning about the world depends upon a principle of conservation that is not itself a product of empirical evidence. This principle can, therefore, be understood as synthetic *a priori*. It is not, however, evident that all objective empirical judgments presuppose a strict physical law of conservation. Nevertheless, in order for us to understand the appearances presented by our intuitions as objective, the flow of those intuitions must involve enough continuity and constancy to enable us to count the appearances as manifestations of changes that are taking place in substances or substance, as the First Analogy claims.

5.4 The Second Analogy: Causation (B232–56)

Like the other Analogies, the Second Analogy is formulated in different ways in the two editions of the *Critique*. In A it reads: "Everything that happens, that is, begins to be, presupposes something upon which it follows according to a rule" (A189). In B it reads: "All alterations take place in conformity with the law of the connection of cause and effect" (B232). There are two main differences between these formulations. The first difference is that, while the A version refers to all *events* (that is, things that happen), the B version refers to all *alterations*, which are changes in something that persists through the changes. This gap is bridged by the First Analogy, which implies that all events are alterations. The second difference is that, while the A version says that all events (or alterations) follow something "according to a rule" the B version says that they "take place in conformity with the law of the connection of cause and effect." This gap can be bridged by noting that Kant holds that particular causal relations presuppose empirical laws of nature that govern them, and that the *rules* he refers to in the A version are empirical laws of nature (see, for example, A126).

In light of Kant's assumptions, the Second Analogy is an application of the principle of causation, *Every event has a cause*, to changes of appearances. Kant also refers to the Second Analogy as "the principle of sufficient reason" and draws attention to its status as a regulative principle concerning "the ground of possible experience, that is, of objective cognition of appearances in respect of their relation in the order of time" (A200–1/B246). The principle's regulative status can be brought out by formulating it as the rule that *a change in appearances should be counted as an objective event only if it can be understood as having a cause*. This should not be taken to suggest that one must be able to identify a cause of any event that one takes to be objective, but only that, in order to count it as objective, one must be committed to its having a cause.

As indicated earlier, the first paragraph in the "Proof" of the Second Analogy is a review of the First Analogy that Kant added to the B edition. The second paragraph (B233–4), which he also added to B, summarizes his main argument in support of the Second Analogy. The core of the argument is as follows. The perception of an event always involves a succession of appearances. But this succession is subjective, for "the *objective relation* of appearances that follow upon one another is not to be determined through mere perception" (B233–4). Hence:

> In order that this [objective] relation be cognized as determined, the relation between the two states must be so thought that it is thereby determined as necessary which of them must be placed before, and which of them after, and that they cannot be placed in the reverse relation. (B234)

The applicable relation is "the *relation cause and effect*, the former of which determines the latter in time, as its consequence" (B234). Given that effects necessarily succeed their causes, applying the concept of cause and effect to the succession of appearances renders the succession determinate and objective rather than arbitrary and subjective. So "Experience itself . . . is . . . possible only in so far as we subject the succession of appearances, and therefore all alteration, to the law of causality" (B234). Notice that if this reasoning is effective, then the principle of causation (or "the law of causality") is a presupposition rather than a product of empirical judgment. So it can be understood as synthetic *a priori*.

Kant unpacks this argument with the help of two examples in the following six paragraphs (A189–95/B234–40). He begins by distinguishing between subjective and objective succession, observing that the mere apprehension of appearances in succession does not settle the question of "Whether they also follow one another in the object" (A189/B234)—that is, objectively. To illustrate this point, Kant contrasts a succession of perceptions of the different parts of a house—or "the manifold in the appearance of a house" (A190/B235)—with a succession of perceptions of a ship floating downstream in a river (see A192/B237). In the case of the house, "my perception could begin with the apprehension of the roof and end with the basement, or could begin below and end above; and I could similarly apprehend the manifold . . . either from right to left or from left to right" (A192/B237–8). Now, while our perception of the manifold of the house is successive, "no one will grant" that "the manifold of the house is also in itself successive" (A190/B235–6)—because it is obvious that the parts of the house coexist. So the appearances of the parts of the house are subjectively successive but not objectively successive. In the case of the ship, in contrast, "My perception of its lower position follows upon the perception of its position higher up in the stream, and it is impossible that in the apprehension of this appearance the ship should first be perceived lower down in the stream and afterwards higher up" (A192/B237). So the appearances of the ship's floating downstream are both subjectively and objectively successive.

How should we account for the difference between cases like the house and cases like the ship's floating downstream? We cannot do so by treating objective succession as succession among things in themselves, because this wrongly implies that things in themselves are in time and that objective succession is completely beyond our grasp (see A190/B235). Kant's alternative is as follows. When I perceive an ongoing particular, such as a house, I do not have to perceive its parts in any determinate order. But when I perceive something that happens, such as a ship's floating downstream in a river, "The order in which the perceptions succeed one another in apprehension is . . . determined" (A192/B237), and thus irreversible. This cannot be a brute fact but is something that requires an explanation. In order to explain it, Kant claims, "we must derive the *subjective succession* of apprehension from the *objective succession* of appearances"; for "Otherwise the order of apprehension is entirely undetermined" (as it is in the case of the house) (A193/B238). But what, then, explains the objective succession? Kant's answer is that "objective succession . . . consist[s] in that order of the manifold of appearance according to which, *in conformity with a rule*, the apprehension of that which happens follows upon the apprehension of that which precedes" (A193/B238). For if an event were not preceded by anything that it must follow according to a rule, then "All succession of perception . . . would be merely subjective" (A194/B239).

Here Kant offers a persuasive explanation of objective succession in the case of events, namely, that it is an order that is determined by causal laws, which he calls *rules*. If so, the order of the appearances of the ship at different points of its movement downstream is objective because it is determined—or necessitated—by causal connections involving the flow of the river, the ship's motion, and its relations to the intuitions of the observer.[4] More generally, Kant is claiming that the position of events in objective time is determined by their position in the order of causation. This is, surely, correct.

After presenting his basic case for the Second Analogy, Kant considers the objection that (as Hume held) we learn about causation on the basis of temporal succession rather than the other way around. Kant expresses the objection as follows:

> This [reasoning] may seem to contradict all that has hitherto been taught in regard to the procedure of our understanding. The accepted view is that only through the perception and comparison of events repeatedly following in a uniform manner upon preceding appearances are we enabled to discover a rule according to which certain events always follow upon certain appearances, and that this is the way in which we are first led to construct for ourselves the concept of cause. (A195/B240-1)

Kant responds to this objection in two steps.

First, he notes that if it were formed in this way, then "the concept [of cause] . . . would be merely empirical, and the rule which it supplies, that everything which happens has a cause, would be as contingent as the experience upon which it is based" (A195-6/B241). So we would not be justified in treating this rule as a necessary *a priori* principle. And it is worth repeating that if the principle of causation is contingent and *a posteriori*, then it is not even clear that we know it to be true, because there are numerous events that we take to have causes even though we cannot identify their causes empirically.

Second, Kant claims that

> [W]e never . . . ascribe succession (that is, the happening of some event which previously did not exist) to the object, and so distinguish it from subjective sequence in our apprehension, except when there is an underlying rule which compels us to observe this order of perceptions rather than any other. (A196/B241-2)

The argument that Kant offers in support of this claim (A197–9/ B242–4) is largely a repetition of his basic argument for the Second Analogy, the core of which can be summarized as follows. Causation involves objective succession rather than mere subjective succession, and objective succession is not given in the empirical contents of a series of perceptions. Judgments of objective succession must, therefore, depend upon something provided by the understanding in terms of which the succession of perceptions can be counted as determinate rather than arbitrary. And this something, Kant claims, is the concept of causation. If so, the idea of objective succession presupposes that of causation rather than the other way round. This is a profoundly interesting and enlightening response to Hume's skepticism about causation.

After reviewing some aspects of his case for the Second Analogy (see A199–202/B244–7), Kant raises a further possible objection— or "difficulty"—namely, that it is possible for a cause and its effect to be simultaneous (see A202/B247). Hume's brief discussion of this possibility helps to illustrate why it should matter to Kant. Hume writes:

> Now, if any cause may be perfectly co-temporary with its effect, 'tis certain . . . that they must all of them be so; since any one of them, which retards its operation for a single moment, exerts not itself at that very individual time, in which it might have operated; and therefore is no proper cause. The consequence of this wou'd be no less than the destruction of that succession of causes, which we observe in the world; and indeed, the utter annihilation of time. For if one cause were co-temporary with its effect, and this effect with *its* effect, and so on, 'tis plain that there wou'd be no such thing as succession, and all objects must be co-existent.[5]

If Hume's thinking is correct, then simultaneous causation would undermine Kant's claim that the objective time-order of events is determined by their position in the order of causation, because events would not occur later than their causes.

Hume takes his breezy reasoning to establish by *reductio ad absurdum* that causes and effects cannot be perfectly co-temporary. Kant discusses the problem of simultaneous causation much more carefully (see A202–9/B247–54). He begins by insisting that there is simultaneous causation in nature in the sense that "in the moment in which the effect first comes to be, it is invariably simultaneous with the causality of its cause," because "If the cause should have ceased to exist a moment before, the effect would never have come to be" (A203/B248). Nevertheless, he goes on to argue that change in nature takes time by appealing to the continuity of both time and the causal processes involved in alterations in the state of a substance (or of substance):

> Between two instants there is always a time, and between any two states in the two instants there is always a difference which has magnitude. . . . All transition from one state to another therefore occurs in a time which is contained between two instants. . . . Now every alteration has a cause which evinces its causality in the whole time in which the alteration takes place. This cause, therefore, does not engender the alteration suddenly, that is, at once or in one instant, but in a time. . . . All alteration is thus only possible through a continuous action of the causality. . . . (A208/B253–4)

It follows that "If a substance passes from one state, a, to another, b, the point of time of the second is distinct from that of the first, and follows upon it" (A207/B253).

Kant's solution to the problem of simultaneous causation can be illustrated with the help of two examples which he uses to introduce the problem. The first is as follows:

> [A] room is warm while the outer air is cool. I look around for the cause, and find a heated stove. Now the stove, as cause, is simultaneous with its effect, the heat of the room. Here there is no serial succession in time between cause and effect. They are simultaneous, and yet the law [of cause and effect] is valid. (A202/B247–8)

Kant does not explain how his solution to the problem applies to this example, but only that what we are considering is "the *order* of time, not the *lapse* of time" because "the relation remains even if no time has elapsed" (A203/B248). But, because the Second Analogy is concerned with relations between events rather than states of affairs (such as the room's being warm), it would be more useful to focus on the *continuous process* of the stove's heat spreading through the room and then maintaining its warmth. As implied by

Kant's general response to the problem of simultaneous causation, this takes time even though the generation of heat in the stove begins at the very instant when the fuel starts burning. (It could not begin later, because at any later time—no matter how short the intervening interval may be—the effect is already in progress.)

After presenting the second example that he uses to introduce the problem, Kant makes some remarks which anticipate but do not reveal his solution:

> If I view as a cause a [leaden] ball which impresses a hollow as it lies on a stuffed cushion, the cause is simultaneous with the effect. But I still distinguish the two through the time-relation of *their dynamical connection.* For if I lay the ball on the cushion, a hollow follows upon the previous flat smooth shape; but if (for any reason) there previously exists a hollow in the cushion, a leaden ball does not follow upon it. (A203/B248, italics added)

The key here is Kant's reference to the "dynamical connection" between the ball and the cushion, namely, the continuous process by which the gravitationally induced movement of the ball brings about the change in the shape of the cushion. Again, this is something that happens over a period of time (albeit a very short period) even though the shape of the cushion begins to change at the very instant when the ball first touches it.

As these cases illustrate, Kant's recognition of simultaneous causation does not undermine the correlation between the direction of time and the direction of causation that he needs in order to defend the Second Analogy.

5.5 The Third Analogy: Community (B256–62)

In the B edition, the Third Analogy says that "All substances, in so far as they can be perceived to coexist in space, are in thoroughgoing reciprocity" (B256). In A it says that "All substances, so far as they coexist, stand in thoroughgoing community, that is, in mutual interaction" (A211). This makes it clear that *reciprocity* signifies mutual interaction. Translators other than Kemp Smith express the

Third Analogy in terms of *simultaneity* rather than *coexistence*,[6] but *coexistence* has the advantage of signaling that what is in question is not something momentary but an overlap between the times at which two or more substances exist. The Third Analogy's status as a regulative principle can be brought out by formulating it as the rule that *substances should be counted as coexisting only if they can be understood as being in mutual interaction.*

Kant gives an overview of his argument for the Third Analogy in the first paragraph of the "Proof," which he added in the B edition. He begins by setting the scene as follows:

Things are coexistent when in empirical intuition the perceptions of them can follow upon one another reciprocally. . . . Thus I can direct my perception first to the moon and then to the earth, or, conversely, first to the earth and then to the moon; and because the perceptions of these objects can follow each other reciprocally, I say that they are coexistent. Now coexistence is the existence of the manifold in one and the same time. But time itself cannot be perceived, and we are not, therefore, in a position to gather, simply from things being set in the same time, that their perceptions can follow each other reciprocally. . . . [A]pprehension would only reveal that the one perception is in the subject when the other is not there, and *vice versa*, but not that the objects are coexistent, . . . and that it is only because they thus coexist that the perceptions are able to follow one another reciprocally. (B257)

In short, the particular time-order in which one perceives two substances such as the moon and the earth cannot show that they coexist in objective time and that they can therefore be perceived in different time-orders.

With this in hand, Kant proceeds as follows:

Consequently, in the case of things which coexist externally to one another, a pure concept of the reciprocal sequence of their determinations is required, if we are to be able . . . to present the coexistence as objective. But the relation of substances in which . . . each substance reciprocally contains the ground of the determinations in the other . . . is that of community or reciprocity. Thus the coexistence of substances in space cannot be cognized in experience save on the assumption of their reciprocal interaction. (B257–8)

So substances can coexist only if they "stand in . . . mutual interaction" (A211).

Something appears to have gone wrong here, because if there is a huge distance in space between two coexisting substances, the requirement of mutual interaction is too demanding. The problem begins with Kant's suggestion that the possibility of perceiving two substances in reversible time-orders is evidence of their coexistence. But because of the finite speed of light,[7] it is possible for someone to see a pen on the table in front of her before seeing a star that ceased to exist millions of years ago or to see the star before seeing the pen. This holds even though the star and the pen do not overlap in objective time and never interact with each other. Kant, however, says something a little later which is relevant to this problem:

Now assuming that in a manifold of substances . . . each of them is completely isolated, that is, that no one acts on any other and receives reciprocal influences in return, I maintain that their *coexistence* would not be an object of a possible perception, and that the existence of one could lead by any path of empirical synthesis to the existence of another. (A212/B258–9)

What this suggests is that any substance that is completely isolated from all others so that it does not have causal connections with any of them cannot be understood to coexist with any of the others.

But this still leaves room for the possibility of two coexistent substances that are not in *mutual interaction* with each other. One possible response to this problem might be that any two coexistent substances, no matter how much they differ in size, are subject to mutual gravitational attraction. I understand that this holds even though it has been established that gravitational forces move at the speed of light, because gravitational attraction is mediated by gravitational fields. This response to the problem has a valuable side benefit, namely, that gravitational attraction is a genuinely mutual interaction rather than a one-way causal relation. But it cannot do justice to the role of perception in Kant's thinking about the Third Analogy, so it is not clear that it can be understood as a condition of the possibility of experience.

Nevertheless, if one substance is completely isolated from all others in the sense that it does not have causal connections with any of them, then there could be no evidence that it stands in any objective temporal relations with the others. This supports a synthetic *a priori* principle according to which substances exist within one and the same objective spatio-temporal system only if they are directly or indirectly linked by causal connections. This principle is much more modest than the Third Analogy, because it does not account for overlaps between the times at which different substances exist, but it constitutes a compelling standard of objectivity that could, for many purposes, replace the Third Analogy as Kant formulates it. It is also worth noting that, even though it is not obvious what further conditions must be added to the principle to explain objective temporal overlaps between substances, it is plausible that these temporal relations are fixed by the myriad of direct and indirect causal relations between the substances. But it does not seem necessary to invoke a special concept of *reciprocity* in order to account for this community between substances.

Nevertheless, if we consider the three Analogies together, we must give Kant full credit for linking the objective spatio-temporal order—and, indeed, objectivity in general—to the order of substance and causation.

5.6 The Postulates: Possibility, Actuality, and Necessity (B265–74 and 279–82)

The Analogies specify necessary conditions of appearances' being objective, but do not on their own provide both necessary and sufficient conditions of appearances' being actual. Kant bridges this gap by means of the second of his Postulates of Empirical Thought in general, which specifies his standard of actuality. In this section we consider all three of the Postulates but focus heavily on the second, which I will discuss after a brief review of the other two.[8]

Kant states his three Postulates as follows:

1. That which agrees with the formal conditions of experience, that is, with the conditions of intuition and of concepts, is *possible*.

2. That which is bound up [or: connects] with the material conditions of experience, that is, with sensation, is *actual*.
3. That which in its connection with the actual is determined in accordance with universal conditions of experience, is (that is, exists as) *necessary*. (A218/B265-6)

Kant begins his explanation of the Postulates by informing us that the categories of modality are not predicates that attribute properties to objects, because "Even when the concept of a thing is quite complete, I can still enquire whether this object is merely possible or is also actual, or if actual, whether it is not also necessary" (A219/B266). Furthermore, he adds that the Postulates themselves "are nothing but explanations of the concepts of . . . [modality] in their empirical employment" and that "they restrict all categories to their merely empirical employment" (A219/B266). So they tell us nothing about possibility, actuality or necessity with respect to things in themselves, which are beyond the reach of experience.

The First Postulate claims that "the *possibility* of things requires that the concept of the things should agree with the formal conditions of an experience in general" (A220/B267). What this means is that, for a hypothetical object to be possible, it must be in time (if it is an inner object) or in both space and time (if it is an outer object), and it must also be subject to the non-modal categories and the corresponding principles—including, in particular, the Analogies. As Kant points out, this implies that a concept of a possible object "must either be cognized *a posteriori* and empirically, or it cannot be cognized at all" (A222/B270). For a concept of an object cannot, according to the First Postulate, be a concept of a possible object unless it is framed in terms of empirical concepts in such a way that the object would satisfy the above conditions.

This implies that a logically possible object—that is, one that can be specified completely (or exhaustively) by a concept that is not logically contradictory—may not be genuinely possible. Indeed, there are logically possible objects that are not, according to Kant, genuinely possible, for example, objects in which there are uncaused events and objects which are causally isolated from everything else. Kant's own examples include that of "A substance which would be permanently present in space, but without filling it" (which is to say that it does not take up any space) (A222/B270). The gap between logically possible and genuinely possible objects is not only significant in its own right but also because it presupposes that there are synthetic *a priori* truths and helps explain why this is the case. To illustrate, the proposition *It is not the case that there are objects in which there are uncaused events* is synthetic, not analytic; but the First Postulate implies that there could not be any such objects; so even though the proposition is synthetic, it is also necessary, and therefore *a priori*.

The Second Postulate claims that a possible object is actual if and only if it is connected with "the material conditions of experience" (A218/B266). As we will see, this means that it must be perceived or be connected with perception through the Analogies of Experience. The Third Postulate adds that an actual object is necessary if and only if its satisfaction of the Second Postulate is required by the conditions of possible experience. But this could not apply to anything empirical; and Kant makes it clear in his discussion of the Third Postulate that anything empirical cannot be absolutely necessary, but only relatively necessary—as an effect is necessary relative to its cause (see A226–30/B279–82).

Our main concern in this section is with the Second Postulate, which is about the application of the modal concept of actuality. To emphasize this principle's regulative status, we could formulate it as the rule that *something should be counted as actual if and only if it is perceived or is connected with perception through the Analogies of Experience.*

Kant elucidates the Second Postulate and explains its application as follows:

> In the *mere concept* of a thing no mark of its existence is to be found. . . . For . . . the perception which supplies the content to the concept is the sole mark of actuality. We can also, however, cognize the existence of the thing prior to its perception . . . if only it be bound up with certain perceptions, in accordance with the principles of their empirical connection (the analogies). For the existence of the thing being thus bound up with our perceptions in a possible experience, we are able in the series of possible perceptions and under the guidance of the analogies to make the transition from our actual perception to the thing in question. Thus from the perception of the attracted iron filings we know of the existence of a magnetic matter pervading all bodies, although

the constitution of our organs cuts us off from all immediate perception of this medium. (A225–6/B272–3)

This passage begins with the observation that we cannot determine that something exists—or is actual—merely by analyzing concepts but must draw on the evidence of perception. In the case of objects in nature, which is what Kant is concerned with, this is entirely reasonable. But he goes on to point out that we can have perceptual evidence that something exists even though we do not perceive it directly. He illustrates this with the case of magnetic fields, which we cannot perceive in their own right but which we can recognize as actual on the basis of perceptual evidence. The evidence which he alludes to in the last sentence of the passage consists of the ways in which iron filings which have been scattered randomly on a table-top move into a distinctive pattern when a bar magnet is moved up underneath the table and held against the bottom of the table-top, and their subsequent movements when the magnet is moved around against the bottom of the table-top. Kant is clearly thinking that we can understand the movements of the iron filings as effects of the movements of the magnet only if we assume that the magnet is surrounded by an imperceptible magnetic field that would not be present in the case of a non-magnetic but otherwise indistinguishable bar of iron; and that we are therefore entitled to accept the existence of magnetic fields. This illustrates how our ordinary empirical reasoning about existence presupposes principles such as Kant's Second Postulate and his Analogies—in this case, the Second Analogy. It also makes it clear that the empirical objects to which Kant is committed are not mere mind-dependent presentations.

5.7 The Unity of Nature (B263–5)

In summing up the Analogies, Kant says that "Our analogies ... portray the unity of nature" and that "Taken together, the analogies ... declare that all appearances lie, and must lie, in *one* nature" (A216/B263). A crucially important part of what he has in mind here is that, taken together, the principles on which we have been focusing in this chapter make an implicit commitment to the objectivity of a unitary spatio-temporal system. For if all objective things and events outside our minds are in space and time and are also connected with our perceptions and with each other as required by the Second Postulate and the Analogies (or suitably reconstructed versions of them), then they must all be in one and the same objective spatio-temporal system that embraces everything in nature.

It is important to recognize that this view of space and time goes way beyond what Kant says about space and time in the Aesthetic, which is not concerned with objectivity. As I interpreted it in Chapter 3, the Aesthetic is committed to the view that the forms of sensibility present a space that embraces an infinity of particular spaces and a time that embraces an infinity of particular times. But the Aesthetic does not provide a way to connect the space and time presented in one empirical intuition with the space and time presented in a distinct empirical intuition, which could well be an intuition of different things in different places and at different times. The Aesthetic also does not provide a way to connect the places and times of things that we perceive with other places and times that also belong to our single, unitary, objective spatio-temporal system. These connections are made by the application of Kant's dynamical principles to appearances. So, while the mere forms of sensibility considered in the Aesthetic do indeed present space and time, the categories and the principles of the Analytic are needed to account for the spatio-temporal unity of objective nature.

To end this chapter, let me add that it does not deal with two very significant passages that Kant added to the Principles in the second edition of the *Critique*: the Refutation of Idealism (B274–9) and the General Note on the System of Principles (B288–94). These passages include Kant's arguments for his thesis that the empirical cognition of oneself in objective time is not possible in the absence of cognition of objects in the outer world. The full significance of this material cannot be appreciated before we consider the Transcendental Deduction and the Paralogisms of Pure Reason (the topics of Chapter 6 and Section 8.2). I will therefore postpone discussing it until Section 9.1.

6

The Transcendental Deduction

Why Intuitions Fall Under Categories

In the Principles, Kant assumes that we are entitled to apply the categories in experience and asks which fundamental synthetic *a priori* principles are connected with this application. But what gives us the right to apply the categories to appearances? This is a good question. Consider the category *cause*. If we abstract from matters of time, this category is the concept of something's *necessitating* something else or, for short, the concept of a *necessary connection*. But, as Hume claimed and Kant accepts, mere sensibility does not present appearances as necessarily connected. Intuitions of events that we take to be causally connected *succeed* one another in time; but no matter how deeply we examine what is empirically given in these intuitions, we won't find a necessary connection. So we cannot justify applying the category of cause empirically. What, then, could justify this application?

The Transcendental Deduction of the Categories is meant to provide an answer not only with respect to causation but with respect to all the categories. Kant often considers these together as if they were one, but the specific categories that he mentions most often are those of *substance* and *cause*. And for good reason, because these are the two that are most puzzling. We've seen why in the case of *cause*. In the case of *substance* the problem is as follows. If we abstract from matters of time and consider only the pure category of substance, it "would mean simply a something which can be thought only as subject, never as a predicate of something else" (A147/B186). And, as Kant goes on to inform us, this information does not tell us what kinds of things the category of substance applies to. It is even unclear how the natural category of substance—which incorporates the information that substances are things that persist through change—can be applied to appearances on the basis of what is empirically given in any series of intuitions. For neither the absolute permanence of ultimate substance nor the relative permanence of an individual substance is empirically given in any such series.[1]

The Transcendental Deduction is the centerpiece of the *Critique of Pure Reason*. It is doubtful that anyone has come to terms completely with everything in the Deduction (as it's customarily abbreviated), and there are many different interpretations and reconstructions of it in the scholarly literature. One commentator describes it as "a botch" but still acknowledges that it is loaded with rich and interesting philosophical ideas.[2] And it is widely recognized that the Deduction contains important insights that have made a huge difference to the philosophical landscape. My goal in this chapter is to make sense of the main lines of Kant's thinking in the Deduction without pursuing many complicating details.

I will focus on the Deduction in B, which Kant divides into two sections. Section I, which consists of §13 and §14 of the *Critique*, coincides largely with Section I of the Deduction in A. This is an introduction that explains what the Deduction is supposed to do, why it is necessary, important and challenging, and how it will be tackled. Section II in B, which consists of §§15–27, completely replaces Sections II and III in A. This is the Transcendental Deduction proper. The B version can be divided into two stages that perform different functions.[3] As I will explain them, the first of these stages (§§15–20) seeks to establish that intuitions—which give us appearances—can belong to a unitary consciousness only if they are subject to the categories, while the second (§§21–27) seeks to establish that our intuitions are so constituted that they can indeed fall under the categories.

6.1 The Challenge (B116–29)

Kant explains the problem that the Deduction is supposed to address in §13. He begins by indicating that he is using the word *deduction* in the juridical sense, according to which a deduction is meant to establish a right rather than a fact (see A84/B116). So the Deduction is meant to establish a right to apply the categories.

Kant thinks that empirical concepts don't require an explicit deduction because they answer to something that is empirically given in intuition (see A84/B116). This clearly holds for relatively simply sensory concepts such as *red* and *round*, but it is not obvious that it applies without qualification to much richer empirical concepts, such as the concept *dog*. The concept *dog* goes beyond anything that can be given empirically in a single intuition or even a series of intuitions, because no series of intuitions presents the relative permanence of a dog, which is, necessarily, an individual substance. Thus, if categories require a deduction, so do rich empirical concepts such as *dog*. But if we could give a deduction of the categories, we could also handle such concepts. So we can reasonably set them aside and concentrate on the question of why Kant thinks that categories—including the category of *substance*—require a deduction.

One reason is that he wants to distinguish the categories from concepts (or pseudo-concepts?) such as *fortune* and *fate*, which are "allowed to circulate by almost universal indulgence," even though we cannot establish a right to apply them (A84/B117). More importantly, categories are *a priori* concepts, so an empirical deduction of them is impossible (A85/B117). We could of course conduct an empirical investigation of how the categories emerge in the development of human psychology, but this would establish only facts about their history not a right to apply them (see A86–7/B118–19). A developmental psychology of the categories is no substitute for a transcendental justification.

The problem of establishing a right to use the categories is much greater, Kant holds, than the problem of establishing a right to use the concepts of *space* and *time*. For, even though these two concepts have *a priori* roots, what they apply to is presented by the forms of intuition (see A88/B120). But the categories are different:

> The categories of the understanding . . . do not present the conditions under which objects are given in intuition. Objects

may, therefore, appear to us without their being under the necessity of being related to the functions of understanding; and understanding need not, therefore, contain their *a priori* conditions. Thus a difficulty such as we did not meet with in the field of sensibility is here encountered, namely, how *subjective conditions of thought* can have *objective validity*, that is, can furnish conditions of the possibility of all cognition of objects. For appearances can certainly be given in intuition independently of functions of the understanding. (A89–90/B122)

So the Deduction must show why intuitions are subject to the categories.

Kant tells us how he plans to tackle this challenge in §14.[4] He begins with a passage reminiscent of his discussion of his Copernican Hypothesis in the Preface (see pp.13–14). But on this occasion he distinguishes between cases in which "the object alone must make the presentation possible" and cases in which "the presentation alone must make the object possible" (A92/B124–5). It is clear that the former applies to empirical presentations (or the empirical contents of presentations), while the latter applies to *a priori* presentations (or the *a priori* contents of presentations). So Kant holds that the categories make the object possible. They do not, however, make the object possible merely as something given by intuition but "as *object of experience*" (A93/B126).

The goal of the Deduction is, therefore, to display the categories as "*a priori* conditions of the possibility of experience" (A94/B126). More specifically, the Deduction aims to establish this:

The objective validity of the categories as *a priori* concepts rests . . . on the fact that . . . through them alone does experience become possible. They relate of necessity and *a priori* to objects of experience, for the reason that only by means of them can any object . . . of experience be thought. (A93/B126)

In the Deduction, Kant accordingly seeks to show that our intuitions are subject to the categories because those intuitions could not otherwise provide us with objects of experience (for reasons explained in the Analogies—see Chapter 5). Kant does not doubt that we have experience of objects but seeks to explain how this experience is possible.

In the last paragraph of §14, Kant describes the categories as "concepts of an object in general, by means of which the intuition of an object is regarded as determined in respect of one of the logical functions of judgment" (B128). This reminder of the relationship between the categories and the forms of judgment which he advanced in the Metaphysical Deduction is timely, because the first stage of the Deduction in B turns on that relationship.

6.2 Apperception and Judgment: Why Intuitions Must Fall Under Categories (B129–43)

Kant begins the main argument of the first stage of the Deduction in B with the assumption that experience is subject to what he calls *the unity of apperception*, which he introduces in §16. Broadly speaking, the term *apperception* signifies self-consciousness or the potential for self-consciousness. Kant distinguishes between empirical apperception and pure apperception (which he also calls *original apperception* and *transcendental apperception*). Empirical apperception occurs when one is aware of a presentation in one's own mind, as when one is conscious of one's intuition of a pen. This is the same as inner sense. The unity of apperception does not involve empirical apperception but pure apperception. This is much harder to explain, but let me try.

Kant holds that all thought and judgment is potentially accessible to self-consciousness in the sense that one cannot think or judge that something is the case unless it is possible to be aware that one is doing so. Hence an animal that is not capable of self-consciousness cannot think in this sense. It may be subject to mental activity, but this is mere "animal cognition" rather than the fully fledged, conscious thinking that is characteristic of human beings. Kant does not, however, claim that *whenever* we think or make a judgment we are conscious of doing so. All that is involved in pure apperception is the potential for such self-consciousness. And this potential, Kant holds, is part and parcel of the thinking itself, not something that is added to it or could be separated from it.

Kant expresses the fundamental claim of §16 by saying that "It must be possible for the 'I think' to accompany all my presentations" (B131). Presentations that are not accessible to my self-consciousness—and so cannot be accompanied by the *I think*—"would be nothing to me" and are therefore, in a sense, not mine (B132; see also A116, including fn.). But all the presentations that are mine in this sense are united in being mine. This raises an important question: *What is it that makes my presentations mine in the sense in which this implies that they are accessible to my self-consciousness?*

One possible answer is that what makes them mine is that they occur *in my mind*. But this is not enough. For, as Kant recognizes in *Anthropology from a Pragmatic Point of View*, there are presentations that occur in human minds which are not accessible to their self-consciousness. As he puts it, "The field of sensuous intuitions and sensations of which we are not conscious, even though we can undoubtedly conclude that we have them—that is, *obscure* presentations in the human being (and thus also in animals)—is immense" (7:135, punctuation adjusted). So obscure presentations in my mind are not mine in the sense that they are accessible to my self-consciousness.

A second possible answer to our question is that presentations that are mine in this sense come with an internal *sign* that they belong to me. The trouble is, they don't. I judge consciously that a certain pen which I see before me is black. But none of the presentations which my judgment includes or depends upon contain marks that label them as mine. There is no *me* or *mine* in my intuition of the pen, my concept of the pen, my concept of black, or in the part of the judgment that connects these two concepts, which is expressed by the word *is*. I *make* the judgment, but I am not presented in any of the presentations that it involves. Hume makes a related point:

> For my part, when I enter most intimately into what I call *myself*, I always stumble on some particular perception or other, of heat or cold, light or shade, love or hatred, pain or pleasure. I never catch *myself* at any time without a perception, and never can observe anything but the perception.[5]

A third possible answer to our question is that I am presented to myself as a sort of container in which all my presentations show up.

But this also won't work, because I have absolutely no awareness of any such container.

So some very straightforward and obvious answers to our question fail. What is Kant's answer? It is that what makes my presentations mine is the fact that (as a subject of thinking) I *do* something with them: *I combine (or "synthesize") them into a unity.* As Kant puts it,

> Only in so far . . . as I can unite a manifold of given presentations *in one consciousness,* is it possible for me to present to myself the *identity of the consciousness in these presentations.* . . . [And] only in so far as I can grasp the manifold of the presentations in one consciousness, do I call them one and all *mine.* For otherwise I should have as many-coloured and diverse a self as I have presentations of which I am conscious. (B133–4)

This rich and interesting thought immediately raises a further question: *How do I combine presentations that are in my mind and thus bring them into my consciousness?*

Kant's ingenious answer, which he advances clearly and explicitly only in §19, is that I do so *by making judgments that link these presentations together.* To illustrate, when I judge that the pen is black, I do this by combining my concept of black with my concept of the pen, which I connect with my intuition of the pen, thereby providing that concept with an object. Kant's account of the unity of apperception implies that I bring these presentations into my consciousness by forming the judgment that the pen is black. More generally, *presentations are brought to the unity of apperception by judgments that involve them.* This link between apperception and judgment is by no means accidental, because the thinking to which the "I think" of pure apperception applies is, in the basic case, making judgments. So to be conscious of oneself as a thinker is to be conscious of oneself as one who makes judgments.

In any event, the unity of apperception is not found, but made— as suggested by Kant's claim in §15 that "of all presentations, *combination* is the only one which cannot be given through objects, . . . [and] cannot be executed save by the subject" (B130). And it involves an original synthesis; hence the title of §16, "*The Original*

Synthetic Unity of Apperception" (B131). With this in hand, we can sum up the core of what Kant claims in §16 as follows. For every conscious human agent, there is a combination of her presentations that constitutes the unity of her consciousness and thus makes those presentations hers. This combination is made, not found: it is produced by spontaneous synthesis (see B132) and "is an affair of the understanding alone" (B134–5), for it is a product of judgment. The analytic truth that my presentations are mine depends upon this synthesis. As Kant expresses the point, "the *analytic* unity of apperception is possible only under the presupposition of a certain *synthetic* unity," namely, the transcendental unity of apperception (B133).[6]

Anticipating §19, Kant also tells us in §16 that understanding "is nothing but the faculty of combining *a priori*, and of bringing the manifold of given presentations under the unity of apperception," and that the unity of apperception is "the highest principle in the whole sphere of human cognition" (B135). He reaffirms this view in the title of §17: "*The Principle of the Synthetic Unity is the Supreme Principle of all Employment of the Understanding*" (B136). §17 is useful mainly insofar as it unpacks some things that are implicit in §16. In particular, Kant informs us that, in order for intuitions to be available to the understanding (which is necessary if we are to make judgments that apply to the world of experience), these intuitions must be included in the synthetic unity of apperception. This holds because human understanding always involves the possibility of a unitary self-consciousness (see B136–7). More specifically,

> [I]t is the unity of consciousness that alone constitutes the relation of presentations to an object, and therefore their objective validity and the fact that they are cognitions; and upon it therefore rests the very possibility of the understanding. (B137)

Kant illustrates the necessity of the unity of consciousness to cognition (in the strict sense—see pp.14–15) by observing that even "the . . . form of outer sensible intuition, space, is not yet cognition" but "supplies only the manifold of *a priori* intuition for a possible cognition" (B137). Moreover:

> The synthetic unity of consciousness is . . . an objective condition of all cognition. It is not merely a condition that I

myself require in cognizing an object, but is a condition under which every intuition must stand in order *to become an object for me.* (B138)

The last clause in this quotation implies that an intuition can present me with an object of experience—that is, an objective appearance (see Section 5.2)—only if the intuition is subject to the synthetic unity of consciousness. So in §18 Kant emphasizes that "The transcendental unity of apperception is . . . entitled *objective*, and must be distinguished from the *subjective* unity of consciousness, which is a *determination of inner sense*" (B139).

In §19, which is crucially important, Kant turns to the nature of judgment. In the first paragraph he tells us that a judgment cannot be explained merely as "the presentation of a relation between two concepts" (B140). Kant's objection to this explanation is that it "does not determine in what the asserted *relation* consists" (B141). In other words, it does not tell us what the supposed relation *is*. As he also notes, the explanation "applies only to *categorical* . . . judgments" (B141) but not to other forms of judgment—or "functions of unity in judgments" (A69/B94)—which involve different relations between concepts.

With this in mind, let us consider the title of §19, which obscurely summarizes the central claim of the section. The title says something about "*The Logical Form of all Judgments*" (B140, bold type added). This might seem odd given that not all judgments have the same form. But all judgments still have *something* in common, namely, that they are judgments. This raises the question of what it is that makes them judgments. The remainder of the title of §19 tells us that, according to Kant, what makes them judgments is that they provide "*the Objective Unity of Apperception of the Concepts which they contain*" (B140). This suggests that Kant holds that each of my judgments brings the concepts and other presentations that it involves into the unity of my apperception. As he puts it a little later, "a judgment is nothing but the manner in which given cognitions are brought to the objective unity of apperception" (B141). If so, different forms of judgments are different ways of bringing presentations to this unity. This is in line with the above account of how I bring presentations in my mind to the unity of my consciousness by making judgments that link them together.

Kant's reference to *"the **Objective** Unity of Apperception"* in the title of §19 (B140, bold type added) points to another crucially important theme in the section, namely, that a judgment is "a relation which is *objectively valid*" as opposed to a relation "according to laws of association" (B142). This is Kant's way of saying that judgments are objective commitments rather than mere associations of presentations. He uses the judgment *Bodies are heavy* to illustrate what he has in mind, claiming that in this judgment the presentations *body* and *heavy* "belong to one another *in virtue of the necessary unity* of apperception in the synthesis of intuitions, that is, according to principles of the objective determination of all presentations, in so far as cognition can be acquired by means of these presentations" (B142). The principles that Kant alludes to here are the dynamical principles (see Chapter 5). So his claim implies that, through synthesis, the judgment that bodies are heavy presents bodies and things that are heavy (i.e., have weight) as connected in the sorts of ways that the dynamical principles require for objectivity.

In §20, Kant draws on material covered earlier in the *Critique* to argue that intuitions can belong to a unitary consciousness only if they are subject to the categories. In telescoped form, this is what he says:

[1] The manifold . . . in a sensible intuition is necessarily subject to the original synthetic unity of apperception. . . . (§17) But that act of understanding by which the manifold of given presentations (be they intuitions or concepts) is brought under one apperception, is the logical function of judgments (cf. §19). All the manifold, therefore, so far as it is given in a single empirical intuition, is *determined* in respect of one of the logical functions of judging, and is thereby brought to one consciousness. [2] Now the *categories* are just these functions of judgment, in so far as they are employed in determination of the manifold of a given intuition. [Kant refers here to §13, but the applicable passage, B128, is in §14.] [3] Consequently, the manifold in a given intuition is necessarily subject to the categories. (B143, reference numerals added)

The core of the argument that Kant advances here is as follows. (1) Intuitions belong to a unitary consciousness only if they are brought there by judgments of some form—or, equivalently, by a logical function of judging. But (2) the categories are "concepts of an object in general, by means of which the intuition of an object is regarded as determined in respect of one of the logical functions of judgment" (B128). Hence (3) intuitions belong to a unitary consciousness only if they are subject to categories. The critical move here is expressed by (1), which treats the self-consciousness of the unity of apperception as inseparable from the object-consciousness that is implicit in the commitments of judgment (for reasons Kant advances in §§17–19). If this holds, then self-consciousness and object-consciousness are two sides of the same coin and are constituted together. This thought is eloquently expressed by the British philosopher Peter Strawson (1919–2006):

> What is required for a series of experiences to belong to a single consciousness is that they should possess precisely that rule-governed connectedness which is also required for them collectively to constitute a temporally extended experience of a single objective world.[7]

I do not think Kant is entitled to claim that he has decisively *proved* that this is the case in the Deduction. But it is an interesting and insightful idea that is supported by the link between the "I think" of apperception and judgment (see p.93); and it provides a reasonable explanation of Kant's claim that intuitions belong to the unity of apperception only if they fall under categories.

6.3 Interlude (B144–9 and 152–9)

Kant begins §21 by reiterating the position he arrived at in §20:

> A manifold, contained in an intuition which I call mine, is presented, by means of the synthesis of the understanding, as belonging to the *necessary* unity of self-consciousness; and this is effected by means of the category. (B144)

It might seem that this should complete the Transcendental Deduction. But a few lines later, Kant claims that at this juncture "a *beginning* is made of a *deduction* of the pure concepts of the understanding" (B144, italics changed). He then goes on to say what he still needs to show—namely, that "from the mode in which the empirical intuition is given in sensibility, . . . its unity is no other than that which the category . . . prescribes" (B144–5). So Kant is now indicating that he has not yet shown that intuitions are so constituted that they are subject to categories, even though he had suggested earlier that the Deduction should do this (A90–1/ B123).

What, then, does Kant think he has established by the end of §20? I believe that the core of what he thinks he has established can be expressed by the conditional claim that *if any intuition is mine in the sense that it belongs to the transcendental unity of my apperception, then it must be subject to the categories.* This conclusion is in line with the thought that the syntheses on which the unity of apperception depends are those that are expressed by the categories, namely, our fundamental concepts of objects and objectivity; and it therefore involves a commitment to a link between subjective and objective consciousness. It does not, however, establish that *all* the intuitions that happen to be in my mind are subject to the categories. What it establishes, rather, is that *only* the intuitions that are subject to the categories are included in the unity of apperception. This leaves open the possibility that *none* of the intuitions in my mind are included in the unity of apperception. If that were the case, then in Kant's terms I would have neither subjective nor objective consciousness. So we cannot just accept that our intuitions are so constituted that they conform to the categories. We should explain why. The main purpose of the second stage of the Deduction in B is to do this by showing that these intuitions involve synthetic unities that are expressed by categories (see B144–5). I advance this interpretation of the two stages of the Deduction as a minimal account which suffices to make sense of why both stages are required but which could also be supplemented in various ways.[8]

In light of the view that the main purpose of the second stage of the Deduction in B is to explain why our intuitions are so constituted that they conform to the categories, the most important passages in the second stage are the first half of §24 (B150–2) and the whole of §26. Most of the other material leading up to §26 consists of comments and clarifications that apply to the Deduction as a whole. Let us take a quick look at some of this other material.

In §§22–23 Kant discusses the distinction between thinking and cognition and their applications. He is concerned with cognition in the strict sense, which includes all possible knowledge. Kant here explains the difference between thinking and cognition as follows:

To *think* an object and to *cognize* an object are . . . by no means the same thing. Cognition involves two factors: first the concept, through which an object in general is thought (the category); and, secondly, the intuition, through which it is given. (B146)

From this Kant infers that any concept without a corresponding intuition "would still indeed be a thought, so far as its form is concerned, but would be without any object, and no cognition of anything would be possible by means of it" (B146). So applying the categories "beyond *our* sensible intuition is of no advantage to us" because "they are then empty" and "are mere forms of thought, without objective reality" (B148; see also B165–66). This echoes Kant's claim in the introduction to the Transcendental Logic that "Thoughts without content are empty" (A51/B75). It also explains why Kant holds that transcendent metaphysics cannot be a science.

Between the middle of §24 and the end of §25, Kant clarifies the difference between inner sense and pure apperception. Most of this passage is a useful appendix to §§16–18. In inner sense "we intuit ourselves only as we are inwardly *affected*" (B153). But "in the synthetic original unity of apperception, I am conscious of myself not as I appear to myself, nor as I am in myself, but only that I am"; and "This *presentation* is a *thought*, not an *intuition*" (B157). Later in the Analytic, Kant adds that "the presentation 'I' is . . . a merely *intellectual* presentation of the self-activity of a thinking subject" (B278, translation of *Selbsttätigkeit* changed from *spontaneity* to *self-activity*).

Before moving on to the second stage of the Transcendental Deduction in B, I would like to set the scene by reviewing some aspects of Kant's discussion of synthesis in the Metaphysical Deduction, as presented in Section 4.4. The key points to which I would like to draw your attention are as follows. First, the contents of intuitions depend upon a synthesis of imagination. This synthesis, Kant says, "unites them to a certain content" (A77–8/B103). To illustrate this thought, I pointed out that a particular intuition can present something as a cat only if it is associated by synthesis with other intuitions which also present things as cats. Second, Kant distinguished between the *imaginative synthesis involved in intuition* and the *synthesis of judgment*. In the second stage of the Transcendental Deduction, he refers to the synthesis of judgment as *intellectual synthesis*. Third, Kant claims that both imaginative and intellectual syntheses can be either *empirical* or *pure*. To illustrate the distinction: the imaginative synthesis involved in the perception of cats and the synthesis of judgment involved in the judgment that some cats are black are empirical; while the imaginative synthesis involved in the perception of a substance of any kind and the forms of intellectual synthesis involved in judgments are pure syntheses. Fourth, I suggested that, in order to make sense of the idea of a pure synthesis of the imagination, we equate it with *a form of empirical synthesis* of the imagination, such as the form of synthesis involved in the perception of any substance. Fifth, Kant claims with respect to pure syntheses that "The same function which gives unity to the various presentations *in a judgment* also gives unity to the . . . synthesis of various presentations *in an intuition*" (B104). This suggests that the forms of imaginative synthesis involved in intuition correspond to the forms of intellectual synthesis involved in judgment in such a way that intuitions fall under categories. This is the central claim of the second stage of the Transcendental Deduction in B.

6.4 Figurative Synthesis: Why Intuitions Can Fall Under Categories (B150–2 and 159–69)

We turn now to Kant's main line of reasoning in the second stage of the Deduction. This reasoning aims to show that intuitions are subject to categories because they involve syntheses of imagination whose unities are expressed by categories. The core of this reasoning appears in §24 and §26, as signaled by their titles: "*The Application of the Categories to Objects of the Senses In General*" (B150) and "*Transcendental Deduction of the Universally Possible Employment in Experience of the Pure Concepts of Understanding*" (B159).

Near the end of the first paragraph of §24, Kant reminds us that the categories "obtain objective reality" by their "application to objects which can be given us in intuition" (B150–1). In the second paragraph, he goes on to claim that intuition itself depends upon an *a priori* synthesis that does not directly involve the application of categories. This is what he says:

> This synthesis of the manifold of sensible intuition, which is possible and necessary *a priori*, may be entitled *figurative* synthesis (*synthesis speciosa*), to distinguish it from the synthesis which is thought in the mere category in respect of the manifold of an intuition in general, and which is entitled combination through the understanding (*synthesis intellectualis*). (B151)

Kant goes on to say that in order for figurative synthesis "to be distinguished from the merely intellectual combination" it should "be called the *transcendental synthesis of imagination*" (B151). This makes it clear that *figurative synthesis* is the same as the *pure synthesis of the imagination*, which he introduced in the Metaphysical Deduction.

Kant attributes figurative synthesis to "the *productive* imagination, to distinguish it from the *reproductive* imagination," which is empirically based (B152). The productive imagination, he claims, "belongs to *sensibility*" inasmuch as "it can give to the concepts of understanding a corresponding intuition" (B151). It does this by means of "its synthesis of intuitions, conforming as it does to *the categories*" (B152). Notice that here, as in the Metaphysical Deduction, Kant goes beyond the Aesthetic in claiming that perception involves imaginative synthesis, which implies that it is not a matter of mere receptivity. But even though he asserts that this synthesis *conforms to* the categories, he also takes care to distinguish figurative synthesis from the synthesis of understanding, which involves the *application of* categories through judgments. So Kant does not compromise his earlier claim that sensibility and understanding are distinct (see Section 4.1).

Kant begins §26 by telling us what he plans to do in this section and how it is connected with material covered earlier. In the Metaphysical Deduction, he says, "the *a priori* origin of the categories has been proved through their complete agreement with the general logical functions of thought" (B159). In the first stage of the Transcendental Deduction, "we have shown their possibility as *a priori* cognitions of objects of an intuition in general" (B159). To complete the Deduction,

> We have now to explain the possibility of cognizing *a priori*, by means of *categories*, whatever objects may *present themselves to our senses*, not indeed in respect of the form of their intuition, but in respect of the laws of their combination, and so, as it were, of prescribing laws to nature. (B159)

The phrase "not indeed in respect of the form of their intuition" is important. It emphasizes that what is to be explained through the categories is *not* the spatio-temporality of appearances as given to us in intuition, but how it is possible for us to cognize appearances under *a priori* laws of nature.[9] It is obvious that the *a priori* laws which Kant has in mind are his fundamental synthetic *a priori* principles—including, in particular, the Analogies of Experience. Kant does not, of course, aim to establish these laws in the Transcendental Deduction. For, as we saw in Chapter 5, he tackles this task later, in the Principles. What he seeks to do here is establish something that is presupposed by his fundamental principles, namely, that intuitions can fall under categories.

With the goal of doing this, Kant introduces what he calls the *"synthesis of apprehension"* (B160) (which he discusses at greater length on A98–100). He explains this synthesis as "that combination of the manifold in an empirical intuition, whereby perception, that is, empirical consciousness of the intuition (as appearance), is possible" (B160). This synthesis, we can assume, is distinct from the synthesis of judgment. So how can it be shown that intuitions arising from the syntheses of apprehension will be so constituted that they fall under categories?

In a footnote, Kant says that "the synthesis of apprehension, which is empirical, *must necessarily be in conformity with* the synthesis of apperception, which is intellectual and is contained in the category completely *a priori*" (B162 fn., italics added). This suggests that the synthesis of apprehension somehow involves the figurative synthesis of §24, because figurative synthesis is the synthesis of intuitions *"conforming . . . to the categories"* (B152). But Kant does not mention figurative synthesis in §26, let alone explain how it is related to the synthesis of apprehension. These two syntheses cannot be identical, because figurative synthesis is *a priori* while the synthesis of apprehension is empirical. So how are they related?

As noted in the last paragraph of Section 6.3, I have proposed that we understand Kant's talk about *a priori* syntheses of the imagination as equivalent to talk about fundamental forms of empirical synthesis, that is, general ways in which presentations can be combined. On this approach, figurative syntheses are fundamental forms of the synthesis of apprehension, and this implies that all instances of the synthesis of apprehension must exemplify figurative syntheses. If so, the synthesis of apprehension will, in light of §24, yield combinations of intuitions that conform to the categories. But why should figurative synthesis conform to the categories? In §24, the only explanation that Kant offers is that "This synthesis is an action of the understanding on the sensibility" (B152). But, taken literally, this claim is not consistent with his claim that figurative synthesis is distinct from intellectual synthesis (see B151). Let us look for further help in §26.

After introducing the synthesis of apprehension in §26, Kant discusses its relevance to the question of how to "explain the possibility of cognizing *a priori*, by means of *categories*, whatever objects may *present themselves to our senses*" (B159). He does this over the course of three paragraphs on B160–3, in which his most important claims appear in the following key passage.

> [The] *unity of synthesis* of the manifold, without or within us, and consequently also a *combination* to which everything that is to be presented as determined in space and time must conform, is given *a priori* as the condition of the synthesis of all *apprehension*—not indeed in, but with these intuitions. This synthetic unity can be no other than the unity of the combination ... in accordance with the categories, in so far as the combination is applied to our *sensible intuition*. (B161)

We may reasonably take this to imply that the synthesis of apprehension in virtue of which any object is to be presented as an occupant of our unitary, objective spatio-temporal system must conform to the categories. This interpretation makes good sense in light of one of the key claims of the Principles, namely, that our presentation of a unitary, objective spatio-temporal system depends upon and arises from the application of Kant's fundamental *a priori* principles—especially the Analogies and the Second Postulate—to appearances (see Section 5.7).

This interpretation of the key passage helps to make sense of both a puzzling assertion that immediately precedes the passage and a significant explanatory footnote attached to that assertion.[10] The assertion is that

> space and time are presented *a priori* not merely as *forms* of sensible intuition, but as themselves *intuitions* which contain a manifold, and therefore are presented with the determination of the *unity* of this manifold. (B160)

The core of Kant's explanation of this assertion in the footnote is as follows:

> Space, presented as *object* . . ., contains more than the mere form of intuition; it also contains *combination* of the manifold, given according to the form of sensibility, in an *intuitive* presentation, so that the *form of intuition* gives only a manifold, [but] the *formal intuition* gives unity of presentation. (B160 fn.)

How can we make sense of this? I believe that in the above context "space, presented as object," is meant to apply primarily to the unitary, objective space of nature. For, as observed in Section 5.7, the Aesthetic does not provide a way to connect the places and times of things presented in different empirical intuitions—or to connect these places and times with other places and times which we do not perceive but which also belong to our single, unitary, objective spatio-temporal system. In the words of the footnote, this requires the "combination" of empirical intuitions. This "combination," we may assume, is brought about by syntheses of imagination. And it is evident that the presentation of a unitary, objective space requires these syntheses to connect appearances in such a way that the categories and principles will apply to them.

This interpretation of the general claims that Kant advances in the key passage is also supported by the two examples with which he goes on to illustrate these claims. The first is that, when I perceive a house, the synthesis of apprehension combines the manifold of my intuitions into a unity which "must completely conform" to "the category of *quantity*" (B163). The second is that, when I perceive the freezing of water, the synthesis of apprehension combines the manifold of intuition (which present "fluidity and solidity") into a unity in virtue of which my perception "is subject to the concept of the *relation* of *effects and causes*" (B163). Both these examples anticipate the Principles chapter and thereby suggest that the synthesis of apprehension must yield intuitions that fall under Kant's categories and principles.

Nevertheless, it is important to emphasize that in the key passage Kant talks about what "*is to be presented* as determined in space and time" (B161, italics added), not about what *is* presented as determined in space and time. And in discussing his examples, he makes a point of referring to unities that "abstract from the form of space" (B162) and "from the constant form of . . . inner intuition, namely, time" (B163). This abstraction from space and time is a sign that in §26 Kant is concerned mainly with the pure categories rather than the natural categories (see p.55). This is appropriate because the natural categories are not supposed to come into play until the following chapter of the *Critique*, namely, the Schematism. So it makes sense to assume that, whatever else Kant is doing in this passage, he is mainly trying to make it plausible that the synthesis of apprehension—and, implicitly, figurative synthesis—must conform to categories.

After discussing the perception of freezing water, Kant restates the puzzle of §26 as the question of "how it can be conceivable that nature should have to proceed in accordance with the categories" (B163). He then informs us that he is going to give "The solution of this seeming enigma" (B163) in the following paragraph, which ends §26. The crucial passage in that paragraph is this:

[I]t is imagination that connects the manifold of sensible intuition; and imagination is dependent for the unity of its intellectual synthesis upon the understanding, and for the manifoldness of apprehension upon sensibility. All possible perception is thus dependent upon synthesis of apprehension, and this empirical synthesis in turn upon transcendental synthesis, and therefore upon the categories. (B164)

But how does the synthesis of imagination depend upon intellectual synthesis? As far as I can tell, Kant does not give a clear and unambiguous answer in the *Critique of Pure Reason*. Longuenesse has, however, advanced the hypothesis that it is the *function* of imaginative syntheses to produce perceptions that conform to the synthesis of understanding and so fall under categories.[11] Setting aside the details of how Longuenesse develops and defends her hypothesis, the great attraction of the hypothesis from our perspective is that it reconciles Kant's claim that the synthesis of apprehension is "*dependent upon* . . . transcendental synthesis, and therefore upon the categories" (B164, italics added) with his claim that the synthesis of imagination is *distinct from* the synthesis of understanding (see B151). For syntheses of imagination are, as Longuenesse puts it, "sensible and preconceptual," and so do not involve the direct application of categories or other discursive concepts. And this holds even though "the function of these syntheses is to generate in the sensible given the forms of unity . . . susceptible to being reflected under concepts"—including, in particular, the categories.

Longuenesse's hypothesis could be subsumed under the broader view that human sensibility and understanding are functionally interdependent, like the organs of a living animal. So, even though sensibility and understanding are distinct capacities, the two of them together constitute a unitary cognitive system, and neither of them would have the same powers in the absence of the other.[12] As I would unpack this position, the functions of imagination include the production of intuitions that are subject to the unity of the understanding and therefore fall under the categories; and the functions of the understanding include the production of concepts that are responsive to the spatiality and temporality of appearances presented by intuitions. Some external evidence for the claim that Kant holds such a view on the unity of cognition appears in the *Critique of Judgment*, in which he mentions "the harmony . . . between the presentation of the object and the lawfulness . . . in the empirical use of the subject's power of judgment" and explains this lawfulness as "the unity between imagination and understanding" (5:190).[13]

Both Longuenesse's hypothesis and the broader view on the unity of cognition explain *why* intuitions fall under categories, but they do not explain *how* intuitions fall under categories. Providing such an explanation is one of the main purposes of the Schematism, which we consider in Chapter 7.

6.5 Dreams, Hallucinations, and Seemings

In a passage in §13 that was cited in Section 5.3, Kant says that he supposes that "Appearances might very well be so constituted that the understanding should not find them to be in accordance with the conditions of its unity" (A90/B123). If so, they would not be subject to categories but "would none the less present objects to our intuition" because "intuition stands in no need whatsoever of the functions of thought" (A90–1/B123). Some commentators have expressed dissatisfaction with this passage on the ground that Kant is committed to denying the possibility of intuitions that are not subject to categories. And, in light of the first stage of the Deduction in B, we must recognize that he is committed to denying the possibility of *conscious* intuitions that are not subject to categories. But it is petty to object to the passage for this reason. For we can reasonably understand the passage as describing a state of affairs that may seem possible on the basis of what has been said in the *Critique* before §13 in order to set the scene for an argument that it is not.

Nevertheless, Kant's commitment to denying the possibility of conscious intuitions that are not subject to the categories raises the question of how he can accommodate dreams and hallucinations. For "the series of appearances" given in a dream or hallucination "might be in such confusion" that "the understanding should not find them to be in accordance with the conditions of its unity," which are expressed by the categories (A90/B123). Dreams and hallucinations can, however, be conscious, as Kant himself recognizes (see B278). But how can he accommodate them? C. I. Lewis expresses this challenge by means of the exclamatory question: "Did the sage of Königsberg have no dreams!"[14]

One possible response might be that not every conscious intuition must be subject to every category, and that the intuitions constituting dreams and hallucinations are not brought to the unity of apperception by relational categories such as *substance* and *cause*, which carry a commitment to objectivity, but by mathematical categories, which do not. The problem with this way out is that, without further qualification, it leaves open the possibility that *all* conscious intuitions could be brought to the unity of apperception by mathematical categories. If so, the categories of *substance* and *cause* would not be required. But these are the categories that are most in need of a justification. For, as Kant tells us in the Principles, the mathematical categories can be applied entirely on the basis of what is given in intuition, and only the dynamical categories go beyond what is given in intuition (see A160–2/B199–202, A178–81/B220–4).

Kant's distinction between mathematical and dynamical categories may be associated with another distinction which he draws in the *Prolegomena* between "mere *judgments of perception*" and "*judgments of experience*" (*Prolegomena* 4:298). Judgments of perception, as described in the *Prolegomena*, are about how things *seem* to the agent—or, as I will say, *seemings*—and "are only subjectively valid"; while judgments of experience "have objective validity" inasmuch as they "always hold good for us and in the same way for everybody else" (*Prolegomena* 4:298). Using this distinction, one could perhaps accommodate conscious dreams and hallucinations—along with conscious seemings—by saying that they are brought to the unity of apperception by judgments of perception rather than judgments of experience. The problem with this way out is that, without further qualifications, it leaves open the possibility that *all* conscious intuitions could be brought to the unity of apperception by judgments of perception. If so, judgments of experience are not required.

In any event, Kant makes it absolutely clear in §19 of the *Critique* that he thinks that what he called "judgments of perception" in the *Prolegomena* are not, after all, judgments. In particular, he insists that "a *judgment*" is "a relation which is *objectively valid*"; and he goes on to say that a judgment "can be distinguished adequately from a relation of the same presentations that would have only subjective validity" (B142). He illustrates the difference by contrasting the judgment that *Bodies are heavy* with the assertion that "If I support a body, I feel an impression of weight," which he takes to have "only subjective validity" (B142). And this assertion clearly expresses what Kant called a "judgment of perception" in the *Prolegomena*.

However, the contrast which Kant needs in both the *Prolegomena* and §19 of the *Critique* is not a contrast between different types of judgments but between, on the one hand, judgments, which make objective commitments, and, on the other, mere associations, or seemings, which do not. This opens up the possibility of applying the term *judgments of perception* to judgments about one's inner sense, and accommodating conscious dreams, hallucinations and seemings by recognizing that they are brought to the unity of apperception by these judgments. I will argue that Kant could accept this possibility without sacrificing his view that the unity of apperception requires judgments of experience. I will do so on the ground that all judgments, including judgments of perception (reinterpreted as judgments about one's inner sense), presuppose judgments of experience. And I will mention important evidence that this accords with the main line of Kant's thinking in the Analytic.

I begin by arguing that all judgments presuppose judgments of experience. The argument is based on Kant's claim that judgment is apperceptive inasmuch as someone cannot make a judgment without being able to recognize that she is making it. This in turn implies that someone cannot make a judgment unless she has the concept of judgment. In other words, she must understand what a judgment *is*. This reflects an important difference between judgments, which involve the exercise of the capacity for reflective thought that is characteristic of human beings, and mere animal beliefs.

Now, in order to understand what a judgment is, one must grasp clearly that judgments are true or false and that they can, therefore, be *in error*. But it is not so easy to acquire a clear understanding of the possibility that one is in error. It appears that very small children and non-human animals do not have such an understanding. And it is plausible that, in order to develop it, one must first be able to recognize that *others* are sometimes in error. And there is empirical evidence that very small children cannot do this.[15]

Following the American philosopher Donald Davidson (1917–2003), I suggest that for someone to develop an understanding of the possibility of error, it is necessary for her to learn a language and acquire the ability to use it to ascribe false beliefs to others.[16] But in order to do this, she requires not only beliefs about what others believe but also beliefs about objective things in the world. And once her capacity for belief becomes a capacity for judgment, she will also make judgments about the objective world that go beyond what is given in intuition. And *these* judgments will, of course, be judgments of experience that involve the application of dynamical categories. From this it follows that *all* judgments—including judgments about oneself and one's intuitions—presuppose judgments of experience. This is in line with Kant's insistence in §18 that the unity of apperception is objective (see B139) and his claim in the Refutation of Idealism (which was added to the B edition) that "the existence of outer things is required for the possibility of a determinate consciousness of the self" (B278).

We turn next to the question of whether judgments of perception, understood as judgments about one's inner sense, are genuine judgments. Kant should accept that they are, because they involve a commitment to objectivity. Lewis White Beck, who advances such an understanding of judgments of perception, explains why:

> While the judgment [of perception] "When I see the sun's shining on the stone I feel the stone's becoming warm" may be true only *of me*, it is not true merely *for me*. It does not say that if *you* see the one *you* will feel the other; but it does say that *you would be right* if you affirmed that when *I* see the one *I* feel the other, and wrong if you denied it. The judgment is subjective in content . . . but objective in its claim to your credence.[17]

And, as Beck's observations about another example suggest, the above first-person judgment of perception is equivalent to a third-person judgment about the agent that is "a judgment of experience about which others can have evidence and on which they must agree if it is true." Actually, I would go further than Beck and allow that a *first-person* judgment of perception could be false, because I think that agents can be in error about their own conscious inner states.

However that may be, it is obvious that the intuitive contents of conscious dreams, hallucinations, and seemings can be expressed in judgments of perception which make objective commitments to the agent and her inner intuitions. But these judgments need not make objective commitments with respect to the outer intuitions of seemingly external things to which her inner intuitions refer, such as my hallucinatory intuitions of a Madonna-like figure dancing on the table. So these outer intuitions need not fall under dynamical categories.

This position is consistent with Kant's insistence on the primacy of the objective, as indicated by the following remark in the Refutation of Idealism:

> From the fact that the existence of outer things is required for the possibility of a determinate consciousness of the self, it does not follow that every intuitive presentation of outer things

involves the existence of these things, for their presentation can very well be the product merely of the imagination (as in dreams and delusions). Such presentation is merely the reproduction of previous outer perceptions, which . . . are possible only through the reality of outer objects. (B278)

So Kant can and does recognize that things presented in our conscious dreams, hallucinations, and seemings need not exist in objective reality.

7

The Schematism

How Intuitions Fall Under Categories (B176–87)

According to Kant, concepts apply to objects (i.e., appearances) through intuitions that fall under those concepts (see Sections 4.2 and 4.4). This holds with respect to all concepts, including categories. But how can intuitions fall under categories if categories are *a priori* concepts without empirical content? Kant addresses this question in the Transcendental Schematism, where he expresses it by asking "How . . . the *subsumption* of intuitions under pure concepts . . . [is] possible" (A138/B177). As I see it, we can find two answers to this question in the Schematism. The first answer, which is fairly explicit and relatively straightforward, provides an account of how the categories are responsive to spatial and temporal features of intuitions. But in certain other respects it is not entirely satisfactory. The second answer, which is suggested rather than worked out, explains how intuitions are so constituted that they can fall under categories. This answer, which is deeper and more insightful, helps to round out Kant's thinking in the second stage of the Transcendental Deduction in B. In discussing these answers, I will restrict my attention to the categories of substance and causation.[1]

7.1 Transcendental Schemata as Criteria

The straightforward answer to the question posed by the Schematism responds to a genuine problem, namely, that there is nothing in the content of *pure categories* which tells us how to apply them to appearances presented by intuitions. For, as noted earlier, the pure categories have only a "purely logical" meaning and have "no meaning which might yield a concept of some object" (A147/B186). So we need criteria to apply categories to appearance. According to the straightforward answer, transcendental (or categorial) schemata are concepts that present these criteria. Schemata, thus understood, bridge the gap between pure categories and what I have called natural categories.

Consider the case of substance. The content of the pure category of substance is *logical subject of predicates*, and it is not at all clear how this applies to appearances. But the category's schema, "permanence of the real in time" (A144/B183),[2] tells us that the category applies to *things with duration in time that persist through change*. Likewise, the pure category of causation is the concept of a *necessary connection* between one thing and another. And its schema, which "consists . . . in the succession of the manifold in so far as that succession is subject to a rule" (A144/B183), tells us that the category applies to *a succession of appearances required by laws of nature*. On this account, a natural category can be analyzed into the pure category and its schema.

There can be no doubt that Kant needs to bridge the gap between pure and natural categories, and that he invokes schemata understood as criteria in order to do so. Not surprisingly, there are interpretations of the Schematism according to which there is nothing more to schemata than this.[3] There is certain textual evidence that supports this position, including Kant's initial discussion of why categories require schemata and his first sketch of what schemata are (see A137–40/B176–9). The applicable claims are as follows. First, to explain how an intuition can be subsumed under a pure category (which has no empirical content), there must be a "mediating presentation" between the pure category and the intuition (A138/B177). Second, "Such a presentation is the *transcendental schema*" (A138/B177). And, third, it takes the form of a "transcendental determination of time" (A139/B178)—which is a reasonable description of the schemata of substance and cause as specified earlier.

But schemata understood as criteria for the application of pure categories to appearances do not explain how intuitions can fall under *natural* categories. This is especially important with respect to the categories of substance and causation. For it is not clear how intuitions can present *things with duration that persist through change* (in the case of substance), or how they can present *a succession of appearances covered by laws of nature* (in the case of causation).

The view that schemata are merely criteria for the application of pure categories also fails to do justice to three important features of the text of the Schematism. First, Kant makes it clear that he is committed not only to transcendental schemata but also to schemata associated with sensible concepts (such as *triangle*) and empirical concepts (such as *dog*), and he spends some time discussing such schemata (see A140–2/B179–B181). Second, he often associates schemata with imagination and imaginative synthesis (see, for example, A140/B179, A141/B180 and A145/B185), thereby linking them with important considerations raised in the Metaphysical Deduction and the Transcendental Deduction (see Sections 4.4 and 6.4). Third, Kant claims that "schematism . . . is an art concealed in the depths of the human soul, whose real modes of activity nature is hardly likely ever to allow us to discover, and to have open to our gaze" (A141/B180–1).[4] This clearly does not apply to schemata understood as criteria. We will consider these themes together in the next section before returning to transcendental schemata.

7.2 Sensible and Empirical Schemata and the Synthesis of Imagination

Kant discusses two sensible schemata, namely, those associated with the concepts *multiplicity* and *triangle*. *Multiplicity* raises no crucial points that cannot be illustrated by means of *triangle*, so I will restrict my attention to the latter, but in doing so I will draw on Kant's treatment of both. On the face of it, Kant thinks that the concept *triangle* requires a schema only because no image of a triangle could do justice to all triangles:

> [I]t is schemata, not images of objects, which underlie our pure sensible concepts. No image could ever be adequate to the concept of a triangle in general. It would never attain that universality of the concept which renders it valid of all triangles, whether right-angled, obtuse-angled, or acute-angled; it would always be limited to a part only of this sphere. (A140–1/B180)

In this passage, Kant completely undermines the imagist account of concepts, according to which concepts are images or traces of images. But the passage does not indicate how a schema serves to explain why so many qualitatively different intuitions can be subsumed under the concept *triangle*—which is necessary to account for the application of the concept to appearances presented by those intuitions (see Section 4.4).

We can, however, move toward such an explanation as follows. In the paragraph before the above passage, Kant tells us that a sensible schema is a "presentation of a universal procedure of imagination in providing an image for a concept" (A140/B179–80). So we may assume that someone who has the schema of *triangle* has the ability to construct images of triangles. Much later, in the Principles, Kant says that

> the formative synthesis through which we construct a triangle in imagination is precisely the same as that which we exercise in the apprehension of an appearance, in making for ourselves an empirical concept of it. (A224/B271)

Given Kant's earlier description of a schema as a "procedure of imagination in providing an image for a concept" (A140/B179–80), we can reasonably assume that "the formative synthesis through which we construct a triangle in imagination" must involve the schema of *triangle*. So the above passage from A224/B271 implies that the schema of *triangle* involves not only the capacity to form images of triangles but also the capacity to recognize triangles and triangle-intuitions. And this is directly relevant to the question of subsumption, for one cannot subsume an intuition under the concept *triangle* without being able to recognize it as a triangle-intuition.

This recognitional capacity must be understood as preconceptual for two important reasons. First, if we exercise the capacity "in making for ourselves an empirical concept" (A224/B271), then the capacity must be distinct from and prior to that concept. Second, if the capacity is to play a role in explaining how intuitions fall under a concept without circularity, then exercising the capacity cannot involve the application of the concept. But can we make sense of the idea of a preconceptual capacity for synthesis that is exercised in both the formation and application of concepts? I think that we can—by means of the following picture, which was foreshadowed briefly in Section 4.4. It will become evident that the details of my initial sketch of this picture apply only to the simplest cases.

Within itself, an isolated intuition is a bare sensation without content. Its having any element of content is not a wholly intrinsic property of the intuition but depends in part on the intuition's being grouped with other actual and possible intuitions (and images) that share the same content. For instance, in order for one of an agent's intuitions to have the content *triangle*—that is, in order for it to present something as a triangle—the agent must at some inchoate level be disposed to place it in a group of relevantly similar intuitions all of which could be described as triangle-intuitions. I do not mean to suggest that she should think about and classify all these intuitions in the same way, but only that she should be disposed to respond to them in appropriately similar ways. Likewise, in order for one of her intuitions to have the content *green*, she must be disposed in the same way to "place" it in another group of similar intuitions, all of which present things as green. So, as Kant puts the point in the Metaphysical Deduction, "synthesis is that which gathers the elements for cognition [in this case, intuitions], and unites them to a certain content" (A77–8/B103). And it is because they have this content that these intuitions fall under certain concepts and thereby provide those concepts with objects.

I would like to emphasize three key points concerning the above picture of preconceptual synthesis. *First*, the syntheses producing the groupings are not voluntary, conscious acts but associative mental processes that occur in the agent's productive imagination. This helps to explain why Kant claims that "schematism . . . is an art concealed in the depths of the human soul" (A141/B180)—and also that imagination is "a blind but indispensable function of the soul . . . of which we are scarcely ever conscious" (A78/B103). *Second*, groupings of intuitions like those that I have mentioned are not based on the recognition of antecedently existing contents but are prerequisites of the intuitions' having content. *Third*, the groupings are not fully determined by the sensations involved in empirical intuitions, because these sensations can be similar in different ways that make a difference in how the intuitions are grouped together by different schemata. For instance, the schema of *triangle* might group intuition x with intuition y but not with intuition z, while the schema of *green* groups x with z but not with y. If so, x and y present triangles, while x and z present green things.

Although such groupings are not completely determined by the sensations involved in empirical intuitions, they do depend fairly directly on these internal features of intuitions. This is enough to make sense of the claim that sensory properties such as being a triangle and being green are given empirically by the matter of our intuitions. This in turn justifies the claim that the schemata associated with these properties and the syntheses that they yield are also empirical.

After discussing the need for schemata for sensory concepts, Kant argues that schemata are also needed for what he calls "empirical concepts," namely, concepts that apply to objects of experience. Here's what he says about them:

> Still less is an object of experience or its image ever adequate to the empirical concept; for this latter always stands in immediate relation to the schema of imagination, as a rule for the determination of our intuition, in accordance with some specific universal concept. The concept "dog" signifies a rule according to which my imagination can delineate the figure of a four-footed animal in a general manner, without limitation to any single determinate figure such as experience, or any possible image that I can present *in concreto*, actually presents. (A141/ B180)

The problem is not merely that the shapes of dogs are more variable than the shapes of, for example, triangles, for this is only a matter of degree. It is far more important that something that is merely dog-shaped may not be a dog but could be something else, such as a stuffed toy or an instantaneous hologram. Among many other things, dogs are individual substances, and the concept *dog* is a substance-concept. Although Kant does not say this explicitly, he implies that the schema of *dog* is "a rule for the determination of our intuition" which reflects this feature of the concept. So the schema of *dog* must incorporate something corresponding to the notion of a substance. But how is this possible?

My proposal is that the schema of *dog* groups certain actual and possible intuitions together in two different ways. First, it places them in a group of relevantly similar intuitions in much the same way as the schema of *triangle*. This in effect makes it the case that those intuitions have the content "dog-like." Second, it segments many of the intuitions in this group of dog-like intuitions into subgroups in such a way that the intuitions belonging to any one of these subgroups could be described as intuitions of *one and the same* dog. In other words, the schema involves *identificatory syntheses*—principled *unifications* of intuitions within the first group. This additional complexity is required because a momentary thing, however dog-like it may be, cannot be a dog. Thus one cannot subsume an intuition under the concept *dog* (and thereby apply the concept to the object given by the intuition) without being disposed at some level to connect this intuition with other actual and possible dog-like intuitions in a way that makes it part of a coherent system of past, present, and anticipated future intuitions which collectively present a single, persisting dog.

Similar accounts of schemata of other types of individual substances—such as the schemata of *cat* and *tree*—are, of course, possible.

7.3 Transcendental Schemata as Forms of Imaginative Synthesis

This brings us to our first transcendental schema, namely, the schema of *individual substance* itself. I will explain how to adapt my picture of the schema of *dog* to accommodate the schema of *individual substance* before offering some textual evidence from the *Critique of Pure Reason* in support of my account.

It is obvious that the schema of *individual substance*, like the schema of *dog*, must involve a disposition to unify various distinct intuitions and thereby treat them as presentations of a single persisting object. But in the case of *individual substance*, the unifying disposition is far more general. For it does not apply only to the intuitions in some restricted group, such as dog-like, cat-like, or tree-like intuitions. Indeed, because there are indefinitely many different kinds of substance (including substances as different as dogs, cats, trees, tables, stars, microchips, and molecules), it must be possible for the unifying disposition involved in the schema of substance to apply to an indefinitely wide range of intuitions (in relation to other actual and possible intuitions).

It is important to appreciate that the identificatory syntheses that this general unifying disposition yields cannot be arbitrary if they are to perform their essential function. This is the function of ensuring that the relevant intuitions have contents that are suitable for the presentation of continuous independent objects and, therefore, that those intuitions fall under the concept *individual substance*. So these syntheses must be systematic and coherent, and conform to appropriate general principles concerning the conditions under which all the members of a given set of intuitions could present a single persisting object. (But we may not be able to specify these principles, which could be beyond our cognitive grasp.)

And there is an important further constraint. It is that the identificatory syntheses produced by the schema of *individual substance* must be completely congruent with those produced by any particular empirical substance-schema. If x and y are the same dog, table, molecule, or whatever, then they must also be the same individual substance. This congruency requirement applies to all actual and possible substance-schemata. For if a certain concept applies to things to which the concept *individual substance* does not also apply, then that concept cannot be a substance-concept. I do not see how the congruency requirement can be satisfied unless the schema of *individual substance* itself shapes and constrains particular substance-schemata. So the schema of *individual substance* does not involve only a general unifying disposition. It must also involve a higher-level disposition to develop only particular substance-schemata that yield identificatory syntheses that are included in its own. So, in short, the schema of *individual substance* is a general *form* of synthesis in virtue of which our empirical intuitions can present persisting objects.

It is important to notice that the schema of *individual substance* does not apply to intuitions on the basis of the qualities of the sensations that they involve but on the basis of structural relations between those intuitions that are determined by the abstract constraints which I have mentioned. So the schema and the corresponding syntheses are *a priori*, not empirical. And the empirical intuitions that present particular individual substances— and so fall under the concept *individual substance*—do this through the *a priori* form of the syntheses they involve rather than on the basis of their empirical matter.

This account of the schema of *individual substance* helps to make sense of views that Kant expresses in several places in the *Critique*. Here are two examples. The first occurs in the Deduction in A, in a passage that does not mention schemata explicitly:

> A pure imagination, which conditions all *a priori* cognition, is . . . one of the fundamental faculties of the human soul. By its means we bring the manifold of intuition . . . into connection with the condition of the necessary unity of pure apperception. . . . The two extremes, namely sensibility and understanding, must stand in necessary connection with each other through the mediation of this transcendental function of imagination, because otherwise the former [sensibility], though indeed yielding appearances, *would supply no objects of empirical cognition*, and consequently no experience. (A124, italics added)

The second occurs in the third chapter of the Analytic of Principles, in a passage that explicitly mentions schemata:

> [T]he employment of a concept involves a function of judgment whereby an object is subsumed under the concept, and so involves at least the formal condition under which something can be given in intuition. *If this condition of judgment (the schema) is lacking, all subsumption becomes impossible. For in that case nothing is given that could be subsumed under the concept.* (A247/B304, italics added)

The crucial implication of each of these passages is that in the absence of transcendental schemata in general, intuitions cannot present objects. There is a certain vagueness here arising from Kant's tendency to lump the categories together and treat them as "concepts of an object in general" (B128). But in the *Prolegomena* Kant says that "the category of substance is the basis of all concepts of actual things" (4:325, fn.). And this in turn suggests that in the absence of the schema of *individual substance* it is impossible for intuitions to present objects as we ordinarily understand them.

In dealing with the two remaining transcendental schemata that we will consider, I will be brief. For the precise details do not make much difference to the claim that transcendental schemata present forms of synthesis.

If there is a schema (or *a priori* form of imaginative synthesis) corresponding to the concept *ultimate substance*, it must involve a preconceptual disposition to treat the general flow of intuitions as a manifestation of a single, permanent, indestructible substrate. This is in line with Kant's claim that "The schema of substance is permanence of the real in time, that is, the presentation of the real as a substrate of empirical determination of time in general, and so as abiding while all else changes" (A144/B183). But it is difficult to get a grip on this schema and its operation, because it is not clear what sorts of syntheses of our intuitions are determined by the schema. So it is possible to doubt that there is a schema of *ultimate substance*. But this is not to deny that we could develop a theoretical concept of *ultimate substance* and apply it to the world of experience.

We come, then, to the schema of *causation*. This schema must involve a systematic disposition to respond to certain ordered pairs of intuitions as instances of a pervasive general pattern which, speaking loosely, brings it about that the first member of any such pair is felt to necessitate the second. This is in line with Kant's claim that "The schema of cause and of the causality of a thing in general, is the real upon which, whenever posited, something else always follows" (A144/B183). The most basic manifestation of this schema is the systematic expectation or anticipation of one type of intuition as a result of the stimulus of another.

On the account of schemata which I have been sketching, a schema in general is a pattern of imaginative synthesis which brings it about that intuitions have the content required for them to fall under a concept corresponding to the schema. An *empirical* schema is a pattern of imaginative synthesis that is responsive to the qualities of the sensations involved in the intuitions which it synthesizes. A *transcendental* schema, in contrast, is not responsive to the particular qualities of the sensations involved in the intuitions but only to structural relations between intuitions. So a transcendental schema is a *form* of imaginative synthesis which brings it about that intuitions have the content required for them to fall under a category corresponding to the schema.

A remark included among Kant's personal notes from the silent decade may help to make sense of this:

> Experience is perception that is understood. . . . Experiences are therefore possible only by means of the presupposition that all appearances belong under titles of the understanding, i.e., in all mere intuition there is magnitude, in all appearance substance and *accidens*, in their alteration cause and effect. . . . The conditions of subsumption under these concepts, however, are derived from the sensible relations, which stand in analogy with the action of the understanding. (*Notes and Fragments*, R4679, 17:664)

According to the account of the Schematism which I am advancing, transcendental schemata are forms of imaginative synthesis that underlie "the sensible relations, which stand in analogy with" the categories.

This account of transcendental schemata complements the Transcendental Deduction by explaining how the synthesis of imagination yields intuitions that fall under categories. In doing this, it also clears the way for the Principles, which we considered in Chapter 5. So, in terms of this account, the Schematism makes a crucially important contribution to the reasoning of the Transcendental Analytic, helping to consolidate Kant's case for the application of his categories and fundamental *a priori* principles to empirical objects (that is, appearances). Notice that one can accept this account of schemata while recognizing that Kant also needs criteria to bridge the gap between pure and natural categories and thus explain how the categories can apply to things in space and time. But to avoid confusion, it is important to distinguish between transcendental schemata as forms of imaginative synthesis and transcendental schemata as criteria for the application of categories.

7.4 An Overview of Kant's Account of Synthetic *a Priori* Knowledge

Recall that in section VI of the Introduction in B Kant identifies the question of how synthetic *a priori* knowledge is possible as "*the proper problem of pure reason*" (B19, italics added). We have now completed our main discussion of Kant's constructive account of how synthetic *a priori* knowledge is possible, which he presents in the Aesthetic and the Analytic. It is time to proceed to his account of the limits of speculative reason, which he presents in the Dialectic. To prepare the ground, let us first recapitulate the most important steps of Kant's constructive account of synthetic *a priori* knowledge as I have interpreted it:

1. Human cognition and knowledge depend upon our faculties of sensibility and understanding. By means of intuition, sensibility provides us with our only access to objects of cognition, while understanding gives us the ability to apply concepts to and make judgments about these objects. (Introduction to the Transcendental Logic and Section I of the Metaphysical Deduction—see Sections 4.1 and 4.2)

2. Such objects of cognition, which Kant calls appearances, must be in space and time—or, in the case of our own mental presentations, which can be presented to us by inner sense, in time—in order for our sensibility to be able to present them to cognition through intuition, because the form of that sensibility is spatio-temporal. So we can know *a priori* that appearances are spatio-temporal. (The Aesthetic—see Chapter 3)

3. Among the concepts that we apply to appearances in cognition are categories, which are fundamental *a priori* concepts that express the fundamental forms of our judgment. (The Metaphysical Deduction §§9–11—see Sections 4.3 and 4.4)

4. All presentations which are fully mine, that is, mine in the sense that they are accessible to my consciousness,

are subject to the *unity of apperception.* This unity is constituted by judgment, for "a judgment is nothing but the manner in which given cognitions are brought to the objective unity of apperception" (B141). So different forms of judgment are different ways of bringing presentations to the unity of apperception, and all intuitions that are fully mine must be involved in objective judgments. Since the categories are conceptual expressions of the fundamental forms of judgment, it follows that all intuitions of which I can be conscious must (*a priori*) fall under the categories. (First stage of the Transcendental Deduction in B—see Section 6.2)

5. But in order for intuitions to fall under categories, they must be constituted by imaginative syntheses that correspond to the intellectual syntheses expressed by categories. Our intuitions satisfy this condition, because human sensibility and understanding are functionally interdependent. In particular, the functions of imagination include the production of intuitions that fall under categories; and the functions of understanding include the production of concepts that are responsive to the spatiality and temporality of appearances presented by intuitions. (Second stage of the Transcendental Deduction in B—see Section 6.4)

6. Transcendental schemata understood as criteria for the application of pure categories explain how categories are responsive to the spatiality and temporality of appearances presented by intuitions; while transcendental schemata understood as forms of imaginative synthesis explain how the imagination can yield intuitions that are subject to natural categories. This consolidates the claim of the second stage of the Transcendental Deduction that appearances are *a priori* subject to the categories. (The Schematism—see Chapter 7)

7. Kant's fundamental principles—including, most importantly, the Analogies—express "conditions of the *possibility of experience*" (A158/B197). In other words, they present presuppositions of all possible experience, which includes

objective empirical judgments and ordinary empirical knowledge. So these principles can be known *a priori*. (The Principles—see Chapter 5)

It should be evident that none of the claims that are presented as *a priori* in this overview are analytic, so they all express synthetic *a priori* judgments. With this in hand, let us proceed to the Dialectic.

8

The Dialectic

The Limits of
Speculative Reason

In the Aesthetic and the Analytic, Kant is concerned with our faculties of sensibility and understanding. In the Transcendental Dialectic (Division II of the Transcendental Logic), he turns his attention to our faculty of reason—the power of systematic thought—which he treats as distinct from the understanding. In the earlier parts of the *Critique*, Kant's main goal was to explain how synthetic *a priori* knowledge of objects of experience is possible, and therefore how there can be a scientific metaphysics of experience. It is reasonable to think that his most important goal in the Dialect is to establish that transcendent metaphysics—a product of pure reason—cannot be a science. This is where Kant challenges traditional metaphysical reasoning concerning the soul, immortality, freedom, and God. He also aims to show how his strictures on transcendent metaphysics make room for an account of human freedom and morality in the domain of practical reasoning, and to establish that, even though the ideas of reason cannot constitute a science, they still have a constructive function in relation to the understanding. Finally, intertwined with his discussion of these themes, Kant develops an account of how traditional metaphysical questions and doctrines arise from the nature of reason itself.[1]

The Dialectic is very long: in the B edition of the *Critique*, it is about the same length as the Preface, the Introduction, the Aesthetic, and the Analytic combined. I devote proportionally much less space to the Dialectic in this introductory book, in which I focus on aspects of the Dialectic that are essential to a basic understanding of Kant's project in the *Critique*. In particular, I concentrate on Kant's explanation of why transcendent metaphysics cannot be a science. But I also explain how this makes room for an account of human freedom and morality in the domain of practical reasoning, and I end with a short section on the constructive function of the ideas of reason in relation to the understanding. Along the way I occasionally mention considerations relevant to Kant's account of how metaphysics arises from the nature of pure reason itself, but I do not tackle this question in its own right because I think it is beyond the reach of an introductory book.

8.1 Ideas and Illusions (B368–75 and 390–3)

The basic negative thesis of the Dialectic is that when we apply our fundamental *a priori* concepts beyond the limits of possible experience, we are driven to illusion because there are no constraints on their application. Kant expresses this thought by means of a striking analogy in the introduction to the *Critique*:

> The light dove, cleaving the air in her free flight, and feeling its resistance, might imagine that its flight would be still easier in empty space. It was thus that Plato left the world of the senses, as setting too narrow limits to the understanding, and ventured out beyond it on the wings of the ideas, in the empty space of the pure understanding. He did not observe that with all his efforts he made no advance—meeting no resistance that might, as it were, serve as a support upon which he could take a stand, to which he could apply his powers, and so set his understanding in motion. (A5/B8–9)

As we have seen, the resistance that Kant depends upon in immanent metaphysics does not arise from the details of actual experience but from the conditions of possible experience. These conditions cannot, however, constrain or support transcendent metaphysics, because it is beyond the reach of all possible experience.

Kant calls the fundamental concepts of pure reason *transcendental ideas*. These correspond to the categories. Indeed, Kant claims at one point that the ideas arise from the categories, because "Reason does not . . . generate any concept" but can only "*free* a concept of *understanding* from the unavoidable limitations of possible experience, and so . . . endeavour to extend it beyond the limits of the empirical" (A408–9/B435). Kant calls the concepts of pure reason (thus understood) *ideas* in order to honor Plato (*c.* 428–347 BCE) for applying his "ideas" (the Platonic forms) not only in the speculative domain but also in the practical domain—that is, the realm of freedom, action, and morality, where Kant thinks such concepts have an important constructive use (see A313–19/B370–5).

He goes on to claim that

All transcendental ideas can . . . be arranged in three classes, the *first* containing the absolute (unconditioned) *unity* of the *thinking subject*, the *second* the absolute *unity of the series of conditions of appearance*, the *third* the absolute *unity of the condition of all objects of thought in general*. (A334/B391)

These three classes of ideas correspond to three important forms of reasoning—categorical reasoning, hypothetical reasoning, and disjunctive reasoning as Kant understands it—and to the three relational categories associated with the forms of judgment central to each of these forms of reasoning, namely, substance, causation, and community. Kant holds that the three classes of ideas also correspond to three major fields of transcendent metaphysics—transcendental psychology, transcendental cosmology, and transcendental theology (see A334–5/B391–2).

The heart of the Dialectic is Book II, which consists of a chapter on what Kant considers to be inevitable illusions within each of these three fields. Chapter I, "The Paralogisms of Pure Reason," is on transcendental psychology, which Kant also describes as "the rational doctrine of the soul," "rational psychology," and "pure psychology" (e.g., at A342/B400, A343/B401, and A345/B403). Chapter II, "The Antinomy of Pure Reason," is on transcendental cosmology. And Chapter III, "The Ideal of Pure Reason," is on transcendental theology. We will give much more attention to the Antinomy than to the Paralogisms and the Ideal, because the Antinomy displays some of the problems that Kant finds in transcendent metaphysics most dramatically by presenting certain reasoning in the field as leading to contradictions or apparent contradictions. But let us begin with the Paralogisms.

8.2 The Paralogisms: The Soul (B399–415 and 421–8)

The word *paralogism* is of Greek origin, combining the prefix *para*—which means either *beside* or *auxiliary to* (as in *paralegal*) or *beyond* (as in *parapsychology* or *paradox = beyond belief*)—and the word *logos*—which means *word, reason,* or *logic.* So a paralogism is reasoning that is beyond justification.

The main goal of the Paralogisms chapter is to show that we cannot draw any legitimate inferences about the nature of the soul from the *I think* of pure apperception (see Section 6.2). Kant pursues this goal mainly by challenging certain arguments from features of the *I think* to important claims about the soul that are widely endorsed by Rationalists. These include the claims that the soul (understood as that which thinks) is a substance, that it is simple, that it is immortal, and that first-person knowledge of it is prior to and does not depend upon knowledge of things in the outer world. The ultimate ground of Kant's challenge is that in pure apperception, as he claimed in the Transcendental Deduction, "I am conscious of myself, not as I appear to myself, nor as I am in myself, *but only that I am*" (B157, italics added). In the Paralogisms he drives this point home by describing the *I* of pure apperception as "the simple, and in itself completely empty, presentation '*I*'" (A345–6/B404). This claim that the *I* of pure apperception is empty alludes to Kant's remark in the introduction to the Transcendental Logic that "Thoughts without content are empty" (A51/B75). Recall that this remark was intended to suggest that, in order to qualify as cognition and thus as possible knowledge, thoughts must refer to objects given by intuition, that is, appearances. So the claim that the *I* of pure apperception is empty implies that it does not refer to any appearance. In the Paralogisms, Kant explains this further by observing that "Through this I or he or it (the thing) which thinks, nothing further is presented than a transcendental subject of the thoughts = X" (A346/B404).[2]

Kant goes on to argue that the *I think* of pure apperception cannot be used to support rational psychology's claims about the soul. These claims are expressed by the four Paralogisms, which are as follows.

1. The soul is *substance*.

2. As regards its quality, it is *simple*.

3. As regards the different times in which it exists, it is numerically identical, that is, *unity* (not plurality).

4. It is in relation to *possible* objects in space.

(A344/B402, converted from a table to a list)

As stated here, the Fourth Paralogism is not at all clear. In the A version of the Paralogisms, Kant indicates that it should be understood as the claim that one has direct access only to one's own soul and therefore that "the existence of all objects of the outer senses is doubtful" (A367).

In the much shorter B version of the Parologisms, Kant focuses heavily on the First Paralogism, which displays the sort of error that he thinks all of them involve. The argument which he challenges is that the soul—"this I . . . which thinks" (A346/B404)—must be a substance because "*A thinking being . . . cannot be thought otherwise than as subject*" and "*That which cannot be thought otherwise as subject . . . is . . . substance*" (B410–11). Kant criticizes this argument on the ground that it involves a fallacy of ambiguity. For the purely logical sense in which "this I . . . which thinks" is (analytically) a subject is different from the sense in which a substance in the world is a subject, namely, an ongoing thing which has properties, can persist through change and is cognizable through intuition.

It is important to recognize that Kant does not deny that there could be empirical reasons for understanding a thinker as an ongoing being but is merely claiming that we cannot determine *a priori* that a thinker is, necessarily, a substance which persists through time entirely on the basis of the *I think* of pure apperception. As Kant puts it, this *I think* "does not mean that I, as *object* [as opposed to thinking subject], am for myself a *self-subsistent* being or *substance*" (B407). Later on he takes this further, claiming that "rational psychology owes its origin simply to misunderstanding" because "The unity of consciousness . . . is here mistaken for an intuition of the subject as object, and the category of substance is then applied to it" (B421–2).[3]

Kant extends his account of what is wrong with the First Paralogism to the other three. With respect to the Second, he argues that from the fact that "the 'I' of apperception, and therefore the 'I' in every act of thought, is *one*" it does not follow that "the thinking 'I' is a *simple* substance" (B407–8, italics changed). For the premise here is an analytic proposition—namely, one which expresses the analytic unity of apperception (see Section 6.2)—while the conclusion is synthetic (see B408); and only an analytic proposition can follow from an analytic proposition. With respect to the Third Paralogism, Kant points out that "The proposition, that in all the manifold of which I am conscious I am identical with myself, is likewise implied in the concepts themselves, and is therefore an analytic proposition" (B408); so it cannot entail that my soul is a substance which maintains its identity over time, because this is synthetic.

With respect to the Fourth Paralogism, Kant observes that from the analytic truth that as a thinking being I am distinct from "other things outside me," I cannot determine "whether this consciousness of myself would be even possible apart from things outside me" (B409). Indeed, in the Paralogisms in A he argues that the empirical cognition of oneself in objective time is *not* possible in the absence of cognition of objects in the outer world (see A381–2). A similar argument is advanced more carefully in two passages added to the B edition of the Principles (B274–9 and B288–94), which replace and improve upon material in the Paralogisms in A. We will consider this argument in Section 9.1.

One of the most significant questions which Kant takes up after challenging the four Paralogisms is that of the immortality of the soul. He considers an argument for this conclusion advanced by Moses Mendelssohn (1729–86), namely, that the soul, being simple (as claimed by the Second Paralogism), must be immortal because something simple "cannot cease to be through *dissolution*" (B413). Against this, Kant argues that, even if we grant that the soul is simple and so cannot be decomposed into parts, it could still have an intensive "degree of reality in respect of all its faculties," which could "diminish through all the infinitely many smaller degrees"

(B414). Hence, even if it were simple, the soul could still "pass out of existence by simply *vanishing*" (B413). This makes sense.

Taking it for granted that we cannot know empirically that the soul is immortal, Kant concludes that we cannot know it at all. He welcomes this conclusion because it leaves open the possibility of "postulating a future life in accordance with the principles of the practical employment of reason" (B424). Likewise, in the Ideal of Pure Reason, Kant welcomes his conclusion that we cannot know that God exists for related reasons. And in the *Critique of Practical Reason* (the second *Critique*), he commits himself to the immortality of the soul and the existence of God, and he assigns them the status of postulates of pure practical reason on the ground that they are "conditions of the necessary object of the will that is determined by [the moral law]" (5:4). These two postulates of practical reason are foreshadowed in the Canon of Pure Reason (Chapter II of the Doctrine of Method—see especially A812–14/B840–42). I am skeptical about the arguments with which Kant supports them in the second *Critique*, but this is not the place to pursue the matter. It is, however, worth noting that they do not play any part in Kant's account of what we ought to do in the major works of the critical period in which he focuses on ethical theory.[4]

8.3 The Antinomy: Nature (B432–48, 525–35, and 556–60)

We turn now to the Antinomy, where four of Kant's categories reappear as *cosmological ideas*. These categories are *unity*, *limit*, *cause*, and *necessity*—one from each of the four groups in the table of categories. What Kant takes these four categories to have in common is that they each involve an indefinite series—or "*regressive* synthesis" (A411/B438)—of possible conditions (see A411–15/B438–42). This clearly applies in the case of *cause*, because whenever one thing is a cause of another, one can ask whether this cause has a cause, and, if it does, whether that cause has a cause, and so on. With respect to *necessity*, something could be necessary, not absolutely but relative to something else, which could be necessary relative to yet something else, and so on. With respect to *unity*, Kant wants to allow for the possibility of a unity being conditioned by more basic unities. He applies this to the whole-part relation so that the unity of a composite unitary whole is conditioned by the unities of its parts, and the unities of those parts are conditioned by the unities of their parts, and so on. With respect to *limit*, Kant is concerned with possible limits to the extent of nature in time and space. He thinks of an earlier time as a condition of a later time and a more distant point in space as a condition of a closer point. This leads to an indefinite series of conditions that will terminate only if nature is limited in time or space (as the case may be).

Kant claims that reason gets into trouble with respect to the cosmological ideas because it demands an unconditioned end to every series of conditions in nature (see A409/B436): a beginning of the world in time and a limit to the space it occupies, simple things to underpin composite wholes, uncaused causes, and necessary things that are not necessitated. (This is an important way in which Kant holds that metaphysics arises from the nature of pure reason.) Kant aims to show not only how pure reason applied beyond the reach of possible experience leads to apparent contradictions but also how to resolve them.

Although his chapter is called "The Antinomy of Pure Reason," as if there were just one Antinomy (or unresolved conflict), there are in fact four Antinomies corresponding to the four cosmological ideas. Kant calls these "First Conflict of Transcendental Ideas," "Second Conflict of Transcendental Ideas," etc. Along with many other commentators, I will call them the First Antinomy, the Second Antinomy, and so on. Each of the four Antinomies is displayed as a pair of conflicting claims—a thesis and an antithesis—in Table 4, an edited version of the table of Antinomies presented in the *Prolegomena* (4:339). Surprisingly, the category behind the First Antinomy (*limit*) is from Kant's second group of categories, while the category behind the Second Antinomy (*unity*) is from his first group of categories. This oddity is, perhaps, a sign that Kant finds it easier to present his thinking by tackling these two Antinomies in the order specified in the table.

The Antinomies correspond to actual disputes in the history of philosophy. These include disputes that are still alive, such as the debate between freedom and determinism, which Kant seeks to resolve in his discussion of the Third Antinomy. Kant introduces the four Antinomies by offering a "Proof" of the thesis and the antitheses of each of them. He later insists that these proofs "are

TABLE 4 *Kant's Table of Antinomies*

1
Thesis
The world has a
beginning in time and
a limit in space.
Antithesis
The world is infinite in
time and space.

2
Thesis
Everything in the
world is constituted of
things that are simple.
Antithesis
Nothing in the world
is simple;
everything is
composite.

3
Thesis
The world contains
things caused
through freedom.
Antithesis
There is no freedom in
the world; every-
thing is determined by
laws of nature.

4
Thesis
In the series of causes in
the world
there is an absolutely
necessary being.
Antithesis
There is nothing
absolutely necessary in
this series; everything is
contingent.

not merely baseless deceptions" (A507/B535), implying that they involve no serious internal errors. He therefore concludes that the conflict between each thesis and the corresponding antithesis which the arguments support "shows . . . that there is a fallacy" in what those arguments presuppose (A507/B535). He identifies the source of the problem as "the supposition that appearances, and the sensible world which comprehends them all, are things in themselves" (A507/B535). We can make sense of what he is getting at as follows.

All the Antinomies concern nature, which is, according to Kant, constituted by appearances, and appearances are objects that can be cognized only through sense, that is, empirically. In other word, appearances are objects that can be perceived or whose existence can be inferred on the basis of their connections with what is perceived—as explained by Kant's fundamental synthetic *a priori* principles, including, most notably, the Analogies and the Second Postulate (see Chapter 5). So any claims about nature are subject to a requirement of empirically cognizability. This makes a difference because there are limits to what we can cognize empirically with respect to an indefinite series of possible conditions in nature. In particular, if we try to work through the indefinite series of possible conditions associated with a cosmological idea, there is no stage at which we can know empirically that we have reached a first, unconditioned member of the series, and there is no stage at which we can know empirically that the regress never terminates and is therefore infinite. This applies to the regresses of appearances with which Kant is concerned because—to repeat the key point—appearances are subject to the requirement of empirical cognizability. It does not apply to things in themselves (whatever they may be) because they are beyond the reach of experience. So when Kant claims that the Antinomies depend upon "the supposition that appearances, and the sensible world which comprehends them all, are things in themselves" (A507/B535), this is equivalent to saying that they depend upon the (false) presupposition that it must be possible to determine empirically whether a regress of appearances involving a cosmological idea terminates or is infinite.

Kant applies this general diagnosis of the source of the conflict in slightly different ways to the four Antinomies. And his resolution of the first two Antinomies—which involve ideas corresponding to the mathematical categories—is structurally different from his resolution of the last two—which involve ideas corresponding to the dynamical categories. In the case of the mathematical Antinomies, Kant argues that both the thesis and the antithesis are *false*. In the case of the dynamical Antinomies, he argues that both the thesis and the antithesis could be *true*, but only *from different perspectives*. More specifically, he claims that the thesis could be true with respect to things in themselves while the antithesis is true with respect to appearances. Kant explains this difference between his resolutions of the mathematical and the dynamical Antinomies by noting that while mathematical ideas apply only to appearances (for reasons that go back to the Aesthetic), dynamical ideas can be applied both within the world of appearance and beyond it (see A531/B559). We will see how this plays out with respect to the four Antinomies in the following four sections.

8.4 The First Antinomy: The Limits of Nature (B454–7 and 545–51)

Does the world necessarily have a beginning in time or outer limits in space? These are the questions raised by Kant's First Antinomy. Let us consider his basic reasoning about time and space separately before we look briefly at the relevance of this reasoning to the Analytic.

With respect to time, the thesis of the First Antinomy claims that the world has a beginning, and the antithesis claims that it has no beginning but is infinite. Kant's "Proofs" of both of these conflicting claims are *reductio ad absurdum* arguments.

The argument for the thesis begins with the assumption that if the world has no beginning in time, then "up to every given moment an eternity has elapsed, and there has passed away in the world an infinite series of successive states of things" (A426/B454). It proceeds as follows.

> [T]he infinity of a series consists in the fact that it can never be completed through successive synthesis. It thus follows that it is impossible for an infinite world-series to have passed away, and that a beginning of the world is therefore a necessary condition of the world's existence. (A426/B454)

The argument for the antithesis depends upon the premise that nothing can arise in an empty time because "no part of such a time possesses . . . a distinguishing condition" which could bring something into existence; and from this it is inferred that the world cannot arise in an empty time, and therefore that it "cannot have a beginning, and is therefore infinite in respect to past time" (A427/

B455). To appreciate what Kant has in mind here, assume that the world came into existence at a certain point in time and ask why it happened at that point rather than at some earlier or later point. This question, Kant claims, cannot have an answer, because there is nothing in empty time that could distinguish the point when the world came into existence from any other point.

Although the arguments for the thesis and the antithesis may not feel quite right, it is not obvious what, if anything, is wrong with them. Indeed, it is easy to imagine someone's finding either one of them enticing. Kant fittingly compares them to the arguments of Zeno of Elea (*c.* 490–*c.* 430 BCE), whose tantalizing paradoxes have had a big impact in philosophy (see A502/B530). Kant does not try to dismantle the arguments because—as in the case of all the Antinomies—he thinks that the proof of the thesis and the proof of the antithesis are internally good arguments. This has been questioned in the literature,[5] but the issue of how good they are is much less important than Kant's response to them, which is to challenge a presupposition that they share. This is the assumption that the world either has a beginning in time or is infinite with respect to past time. It's not difficult to see that if this assumption is incorrect, then both the thesis and the antithesis are false.

Kant holds that the assumption applies the category *limit* beyond the reach of possible experience. Within experience we can approach a limit to a series of conditions through "an indeterminately continued regress *(in indefinitum)*" (A518/B546). But we cannot "say that the regress . . . proceeds *to infinity*" in earlier time (A520/548). And we also "cannot say that the regress is *finite*" (A520/548), because "we can have *no experience of an absolute limit*" (A517/B545), that is, of a point in time when the world began. The reason is that an experience of this absolute limit would have to include both the initial state of the world and the preceding void. But the preceding void is nothing and therefore cannot be an appearance that is reached by a regress based on experience. So it cannot be established that the world of experience—the phenomenal world—has a beginning and it cannot be established that it is infinite.

One may well wonder whether Kant's reasoning is undermined by claims in physics about the age of the universe, which suggest that the world has a beginning. These claims are estimates of the time that has elapsed since the Big Bang, and they are based on observations and laws of nature which underlie the Bing Bang model of the observable universe. According to this model, the Big Bang is a unique event at the limit of an empirical regress. But the model does not imply that there was an empty time before the Big Bang, while the thesis of the First Antinomy implies that there was an empty time before the beginning of the world. So physicists' claims about the age of the universe are consistent with Kant's response to the First Antinomy.

There is also another important reason why physicists' claims about the age of the universe are consistent with Kant's response to the First Antinomy, namely, that these claims are *empirical hypotheses*, while Kant is considering the thesis and antithesis as *metaphysical claims*, which must be understood as *a priori* and thus necessary. In keeping with this, the arguments that Kant offers for the thesis and the antithesis on behalf of transcendent metaphysics do not depend upon empirical claims. The same applies to his response to the Antinomy, for he implicitly rejects the thesis, the antithesis, and the assumption that the world either has a beginning or is infinite *as necessary judgments*.

But isn't this assumption analytic, and therefore necessary? After all, in presenting the "Proofs" of the thesis and antithesis, Kant treats it as equivalent to the proposition *Either the world has a beginning or it does not have a beginning*. This seems to be an instance of the law of the excluded middle, a logical principle according to which any proposition either holds or does not hold. But, although the law of the excluded middle is a principle of classical logic, it is subject to dispute and is rejected by intuitionistic logic—which has important roots in Kant's conception of mathematical proof. This opens up the possibility of dropping the law of the excluded middle and treating the world as indeterminate with respect to whether it has a beginning. But it is not necessary to do this in order to save Kant in the case at hand. The reason is that in the Antinomies Kant is concerned with *the world of experience*, which is equivalent to *the world insofar as we can cognize it*. In this light, the assumption that Kant rejects as a necessary truth is equivalent to the proposition *Insofar as we can cognize the world, it has a beginning or it does not have a beginning*. This proposition is definitely not an instance of a law of logic. And Kant can reasonably deny that it is necessary on the ground that we cannot show either that the regress of experience must have an "*absolute limit*" (A517/B545) or that it necessarily "proceeds *to infinity*" (A520/B548). So he is entitled to claim that neither the thesis nor the antithesis is a necessary truth.

With respect to space, the thesis of the First Antinomy claims that the world has an outer limit and the antithesis claims that it has no such limit but is infinite. Once again, Kant's "Proofs" of these conflicting claims are *reductio ad absurdum* arguments.

The core of the argument for the thesis is as follows. The only way in which we can think of the magnitude of "a quantum which is not given in intuition as within certain limits" is "through a synthesis that is brought to completion through repeated addition of unit to unit" (A427–8/B455–6). But no infinite synthesis can be completed. Thus "An infinite aggregate of actual things cannot . . . be viewed as given whole"; so "The world is . . . as regards extension in space, not infinite, but is enclosed within limits" (A428/B456).

The argument for the antithesis depends on the premise that if the world is limited and finite, then it "exists in an empty space which is unlimited" (A428/B456). The argument proceeds as follows:

> Things will therefore not only be related *in space* but also related *to space*. Now since the world is an absolute whole beyond which there is no object of intuition, and therefore no correlate with which the world stands in relation, the relation of the world to empty space would be a relation of it to no *object*. But such a relation . . . is nothing. The world cannot, therefore, be limited in space; that is, it is infinite in respect of extension. (A428–9/B456–7)

Here Kant tacitly endorses Leibniz's view that spatial locations of things—that is, their positions in space—depend entirely upon their spatial relations to other things (see also A439/B459). This makes sense not only because we identify the positions of things on the basis of their spatial relations to other things but also because the idea that the world of experience as a whole could have a different position in absolute space without any changes in the spatial relations between things within the world is not intelligible. What difference could there be between the world's being located where it is, its being located 100 miles off in one direction, and its being located 43 inches off in another direction (without any differences whatever in the spatial relations between things within it)?

The heart of Kant's response to this conflict is, once again, to challenge a presupposition which the arguments for the thesis and antithesis share. In this case, the presupposition is that it is necessary that the world is either limited in space or infinite in space. If this assumption is incorrect, then both the thesis and the antithesis, which are advanced as necessary propositions, are false. Kant claims that this assumption also applies the category *limit* beyond the reach of possible experience. For, within experience, we cannot determine that a series of ever-more-distant things in space terminates, because we cannot experience an absolute limit to them; and we also cannot determine that this series continues to infinity, because an infinite synthesis cannot be completed (see A517–23/ B545–51).

Once again, someone may wonder whether the assumption that Kant rejects—which he treats as equivalent to the proposition *Either the world is limited in space or it is not limited in space* in his presentations of the "Proofs" of the thesis and the antithesis—is an instance of the law of the excluded middle and is, therefore, necessary. But this is not the case, because Kant is concerned with the world of experience, or the world insofar as we can cognize it. So the assumption that Kant is rejecting as a necessary truth is equivalent to the proposition *Insofar as we can cognize the world, it is limited in space or it is not limited in space*, which is not a law of logic. And Kant can reasonably deny that is necessary for the reasons mentioned here.

Kant's discussion of the First Antinomy is not only of interest in its own right but also because it is here that Kant puts the final touches to his account of the unity of space and time in nature. Let us review Kant's development of that account in the Aesthetic and the Analytic.

In the Aesthetic, our presentations of space and time show up merely as *a priori* forms of intuition. These forms of intuition present a space containing an infinity of particular spaces and a time containing an infinity of particular times. But the Aesthetic does not itself provide ways to connect the places and times of things perceived through distinct empirical intuitions, or to connect these places and times with those of other things in nature that we do not perceive. Kant deals with this issue in the Principles chapter, which presupposes that intuitions can fall under categories. But is not at all clear from the Aesthetic how intuitions can fall under categories. Kant explains how this is possible in some of the most challenging parts of the Metaphysical Deduction, the Transcendental Deduction, and the Schematism (see Sections 4.4, 6.3, 7.2, and 7.3). Then, in the Principles, he uses the Analogies of Experience and the Second Postulate to explain how we connect the places and times of things perceived through distinct empirical intuitions with one another and with the places and times of other things in nature that we do not perceive but of which we have empirical evidence. He also explains how this gives rise to the cognition of things within a single, unitary and objective spatio-temporal system, which is the framework of our world (see Section 5.7).

These connections are made by means of the progressions of empirical syntheses that Kant is concerned with in his discussion of the First Antinomy. And in the First Antinomy, Kant adds one crucially important point that is implicit in the Analytic but is not emphasized there—namely, that these progressions of empirical syntheses can never be understood as complete. But, as we will see in Section 8.9, Kant holds that the transcendental ideas have the regulative function of directing the understanding to seek to extend the progressions indefinitely, thereby broadening their application as far as possible.

8.5 The Second Antinomy: The Divisibility of Substance (B462–5 and 551–5)

The Second Antinomy is concerned with the question of whether composite substances in nature necessarily have simple parts. The thesis asserts that "Every composite substance in the world is made up of simple parts, and nothing anywhere exists save the simple or what is composed of the simple" (A434/B462), while the antithesis asserts that "No composite thing in the world is made up of simple parts, and there nowhere exists in the world anything simple" (A435/B463). A composite thing is one that has parts, while a simple thing has no parts. So the antithesis implies that everything in the world has parts, including the parts of its immediate parts, the parts of their immediate parts, and so on to infinity—or, in short, that all things in the world are infinitely divisible. It is important to recognize that there is no logical contradiction in this thought (even though some may at first find it difficult to get their heads around it).

The core of Kant's "Proof" of the thesis is as follows. If "composite substances are not made up of simple parts" and "all composition be . . . removed in thought, . . . nothing at all . . . will remain" (A434/B462)—not even the composite substances one started with. This argument is motivated by the thoughts that a composite thing depends upon its parts, but that a substance is something that does not depend upon anything else, which suggests that a substance cannot be composite. Kant elaborates on this thought, saying that "composition, as applied to substances, is only an accidental relation . . . [without] which they must still persist as self-subsistent beings" (A435/B463). So "the things in the world are all, without exception, simple beings" and "composition is merely an external state of these beings" (A436/B464).

Kant's "Proof" of the antithesis depends upon the assumption that substances in nature are appearances in space. The argument for the first part of the antithesis—"No composite thing in the world is made up of simple parts"—is as follows (A435/B463). Because "all composition of substances . . . is possible only in space," the parts of a composite substance must occupy parts of space. But the parts of space are spaces, which are infinitely divisible into further spaces (as noted in the Aesthetic) and "everything real, which occupies a space, contains in itself a manifold of constituents external to one another, and is therefore composite"; so the concept of a simple substance is self-contradictory. The argument for the second part of the antithesis—that "there nowhere exists in the world anything simple"(A435/B463)—is that "the existence of the absolutely simple cannot be established by any experience or perception. . .; and that . . . [it] is therefore a mere idea" (A437/B465). But, as we will see, this anticipates Kant's resolution of the Antinomy, which is better understood as the direct conflict between the thesis and the first part of the antithesis.

As in the case of the First Antinomy, the question of whether Kant's "Proofs" of the thesis and the antithesis are good arguments is much less important than his response to them, which is to challenge a presupposition which they share, namely, that things in the world must either have simple parts or be infinitely divisible. If this assumption is incorrect, then both the thesis and the antithesis, which are advanced as necessary propositions, are false. Kant claims that the assumption applies the concept of *divisibility* beyond the reach of possible experience. For, within experience, we cannot (as Kant observes in connection with the second part of the antithesis) determine that a series of parts of things in space ever terminates; and we also cannot determine that such a series continues to infinity, because an infinite division cannot be completed. So neither the thesis nor the antithesis holds.

As in the case of the assumptions involved in the First Antinomy, one may wonder whether the assumption at play in the Second Antinomy can be reduced to an instance of the law of the excluded middle. For, in presenting the "Proofs" of the thesis and the antithesis, Kant treats this assumption as equivalent to the proposition *Either every substance in the world is infinitely divisible or it is not infinitely divisible* (in which the first disjunct expresses the antithesis and the second expresses the thesis). In this case there is, however, a third logical possibility, namely, that some substances are infinitely divisible while others are not. But this is a quibble that we could avoid by considering the alternative proposition *Every substance in the world is either infinitely divisible or it is not*, which Kant implicitly rejects even though it may seem to be a logical truth arising from the law of the excluded middle. However, as in the case of the First Antinomy, Kant is concerned with the world of experience—or the world insofar as we can cognize it. From this perspective, his rejection of the above proposition as a necessary truth is equivalent to a rejection of the proposition *Insofar as we can cognize any substance in the world, it is either infinitely divisible or it is not infinitely divisible*. This is not a law of logic, and Kant can reasonably reject it on the ground that experience cannot determine that a potentially indefinite series of parts of things in space ever continues to infinity or that it terminates in simple things.

Given what I've said so far, Kant's resolution of the Second Antinomy is parallel to his resolution of the First. But Kant identifies an important difference between the two. For while an intuition of anything in space and time does not include intuitions of all things outside it in space or before it in time (with which the First Antinomy is concerned), an intuition of a substance in space at a time does include intuitions of its spatial parts (which is relevant to the Second Antinomy because it is concerned with the part-whole relation). Recognizing this difference, Kant claims that the parts of a substance presented within an intuition are "one and all given together," and so cannot be called an indefinite regress, or "a regress *in indefinitum*" (A524/B552). Nevertheless, he insists that we are not entitled to claim that the intuition of a substance "*is made up of infinitely many parts*" because "*the whole division*" of the substance into parts is not contained within the intuition, which presents them merely as "an *aggregate*" (A524/B552). The division that yields the series of parts of the substance is, rather, a "continuous decomposition" (A524/B552) which, Kant implies, is never complete even though space is infinitely divisible. This infinite divisibility "undoubtedly applies to the subdivision of an appearance, *viewed as a mere filling of space*," but it does not apply to a structured whole in which a series of parts are "definitely distinguished . . . from one another" (A526/B554, italics added).

To appreciate what Kant has in mind here, consider an individual substance in nature, for example, an owl. Not everything that fills part of the space occupied by the owl at a particular time is a unitary part of the owl, such as its heart, a particular muscle in its heart, the outer layer of the muscle, the long fibers of nerve cells, the individual cells, their constituents, the constituents of those constituents, and so on. For example, an arbitrary space within the owl may be occupied by a quantity of matter that includes incomplete parts of the owl's heart, ribs, breast feathers, and other matter between them. But all this material is, in Kant's words, "a mere filling of space," not a part of the owl, which is made up of a structured series of unitary constituents. As this illustrates, the mere subdivision of the matter of a substance in space does not yield a structured series of its parts as such. This series is revealed, rather, by a progressive empirical analysis that could continue indefinitely. The force of Kant's response to the Second Antinomy is that experience cannot show that this analytical regress must terminate or that it must proceed to infinity.

8.6 The Third Antinomy: Freedom and the Laws of Nature (B472–5 and 560–86)

The thesis of the Third Antinomy claims that "Causality in accordance with laws of nature is not the only causality," and that "it is necessary to assume there is also another causality, that of freedom" (A444/B472). The antithesis claims that "There is no freedom; [and] everything in the world takes place solely in accordance with laws of nature" (A445/B473).

The core of Kant's "Proof" of the thesis is as follows. If "there is no other causality than that in accordance with laws of nature," then "everything which *takes place* presupposes a preceding state," which itself presupposes a preceding state, and so on (A444/B472). Because everything in this series is contingent on something earlier, nothing in the series has a cause that is "*sufficiently* determined *a priori*"; but "the law of nature is just this, that nothing takes place without a cause *sufficiently* determined *a priori*"; so we "must . . . assume a causality through which something takes place, the cause of which is not itself determined, in accordance with necessary laws, by another cause antecedent to it" (A446/B474). This is spontaneous causality through freedom.

The core of Kant's "Proof" of the antithesis is as follows. If "there is freedom . . . as a special kind of causality in accordance with which the events in the world can have come about," then some series of events will "have its absolute beginning in this spontaneity" (A445/B473). Now "every beginning of action presupposes a state of the not yet acting cause," and in the case of spontaneous causality, this cause could not be the result of a preceding state (A445/B473). But this "stands opposed to the law of causality" (i.e., the Second Analogy), on which the unity of experience depends (A445/B473). So there cannot be causality through freedom.

Kant resolves the Third Antinomy by recognizing the possibility of both causality according to nature and causality from freedom and seeks to avoid a conflict between them by restricting them to different domains. Causality according to nature, he claims, "is the connection *in the sensible world* of one state with a preceding state on which it follows according to a rule" (A532/B560, italics added). He explains causality from freedom as follows:

By freedom, . . . I understand the power of beginning a state *spontaneously*. Such causality will not, therefore, itself stand under another cause. . . . Freedom, in this sense, is a *pure transcendental idea* which . . . *contains nothing borrowed from experience*, and which . . . *refers to an object that cannot be determined or given in any experience.* (A533/B561, italics changed)

So a cause according to nature is an appearance, while a cause from freedom—which Kant also calls an *intelligible cause*—is not an appearance but a thing in itself, which is outside "the series of empirical conditions" (A537/B565). Hence an action with an intelligible cause "may be regarded as free in respect of its intelligible cause, and at the same time in respect of appearances as resulting from [empirical conditions] according to the necessity of nature" (A537/B565).

Kant holds that "the practical concept of freedom is based on this *transcendental* idea," and that "Freedom in the practical sense is the will's independence of coercion through sensuous impulses" (A533–4/B561–2). So practical freedom, according to Kant, is the power to resist one's "sensuous impulses"—that is, one's desires, fears, and other inclinations—when deciding what to do and doing it. This freedom of action, Kant understandably holds, is presupposed by morality—or, as he put the point in the second *Critique*, it is "the condition of the moral law" (5:4). This postulate of practical reason, unlike the postulates of God and immortality (see p.133), is crucial to Kant's accounts of what we ought to do.

Kant's response to the Third Antinomy raises an important question: If freedom belongs to the domain of things in themselves, how can it apply to human beings, who exist in nature? His reply is that appearances and things in themselves can be identical, and that this holds with respect to human beings. This may come as a surprise because, to keep things simple, I have often (like Kant himself) talked as if things in themselves are always distinct from appearances. But the possibility that some things in themselves are identical with appearances is suggested by several of Kant's locutions, such as "the distinction . . . between things as objects of experience and *those same things* as things in themselves" (Bxxvii, italics added); "what the things which appear to us may be in themselves" (A277/B333); and "things . . . as they are in themselves" (A566/B594). This possibility is also consistent with the way in which I introduced things in themselves, namely, as "objects that we could not possibly experience and objects insofar as they are beyond the reach of all possible human experience" (pp.11–12). This leaves open the possibility of both things in themselves that are not identical to appearances (such as Leibnizian monads) and things in themselves that are identical to appearances. This contrasts with the two standard accounts of things in themselves. According to the "two worlds" account, things in themselves are always distinct from appearances.[6] According to the "two aspects" account, things in themselves and appearances are always identical, and the distinction between them amounts to a distinction between different aspects of the same objects.[7] But it appears that Kant intends each of these accounts to apply to a different set of possible things in themselves.

Now, if an appearance and a thing in itself are one and the same object, then the supposed distinction between the appearance and the thing in itself must amount to a distinction between different aspects of that object. We can associate these different aspects of the object with different ways of considering it. When we consider it as an appearance (or a phenomenon), we are concerned with features of the object that are accessible through sensibility by means of the sorts of connections that are covered by Kant's principles of experience. In other words, we are concerned with features that can be investigated within science. When we consider the object as a thing in itself (or a noumenon), we are concerned with features of the object which are not accessible through experience or open to scientific investigation, but which can be thought only through reason.

Kant applies these considerations to human beings and their conceptions of themselves:

> Only the human being, who cognizes all the rest of nature solely through the senses, cognizes himself also through pure apperception; and this, indeed, in acts and inner determinations which he cannot regard as impressions of the senses. He is thus to himself, on the one hand phenomenon, and on the other hand, in respect of certain faculties the action of which cannot be ascribed to the receptivity of sensibility, a purely intelligible object. (A546–7/B574–5, translation of *Allein der Mensch* changed from "Man, however" to "Only the human being")

So Kant is committed to the view that human beings have both phenomenal and noumenal aspects. The phenomenal aspects of human beings are those that are accessible to the understanding, which is concerned only with "what is, what has been, or what will be" in nature (A547/B575) and is therefore open to scientific investigation. The noumenal aspects of human beings are those that are not accessible to the understanding but are subject to reason—including, in particular, practical reason, which is not concerned with *what is*, but with *what ought to be* (see A547–8/B575–6).

Kant's resolution of the Third Antinomy may now be summarized as follows. From the phenomenal perspective that we adopt when attempting to discover truths about nature, the antithesis is true: there are no uncaused causes. But from the noumenal perspective that we adopt when deciding, acting, and evaluating actions, we are not concerned with actions as mere events arising from natural causes but as products of choices, which Kant presents as causes from freedom. So from this noumenal perspective, the thesis is true: there is causality from freedom.

Kant is onto something important here. Moral reasoning—and normative reasoning in general—is not a form of scientific thinking and cannot be reduced to scientific thinking.[8] At the same time, normative reasoning does not compete with scientific thinking. In other words, it should never (either in its own right or in combination with science) yield conclusions about the subject matter of science that are beyond the reach of science on its own—or conclusions that contradict those of science. This matters. Although normative reasoning goes beyond science, it also depends upon factual claims that fall within the domain of science. So if it yields conclusions that contradict those of science, it is in danger of undermining itself. Be that as it may, normative reasoning is not a form of scientific thinking. And if the concept of freedom is inseparable from normative concepts such as *responsibility*, then reasoning about freedom is normative, not scientific.

Nevertheless, it seems to me that Kant need not invoke things in themselves in order to do justice to the claim that normative reasoning—or noumenal reasoning about what ought to be—goes beyond phenomenal thinking about matters of fact. At one point in his discussion of freedom in the *Grounding for the Metaphysics of Morals* (which draws considerably on the Third Antinomy), Kant says that "The concept of an intelligible world is . . . *only a point of view* which reason sees itself compelled to take outside of appearances in order to think of itself as practical" (4:458). As

Allison observes, "this is difficult to reconcile with the view that
... the intelligible world ... is to be understood metaphysically as
referring to a distinct realm of being."[9] Moreover, it is unnecessary
for Kant to ascribe free actions to things in themselves. For if
attributions of free action depend upon normative reasoning and
cannot be advanced entirely on the basis of phenomenal reasoning,
it does not matter whether scientifically describable aspects of any
free action are caused according to laws of nature by preceding state
and events—providing the action *described as an action* does not
fall under these laws. Admittedly, this does not in itself provide an
explanation of how free action is possible, but ascribing free action
to things in themselves, which are not in space or time, does not do
so either.

To conclude this section, I would like to emphasize that Kant
does not claim to show that freedom exists in his response to the
Third Antinomy. That is a task to be undertaken in the *Critique of
Practical Reason*, for which the Third Antinomy and the Canon of
Pure Reason (see especially A797–804/825–832) prepare the way.
What Kant aims to show in the Third Antinomy is that, although
science and metaphysics leave open the possibility of freedom,
they cannot establish its existence. So isn't it an illusion? Not at all.
The illusion is to think that they have the authority to pronounce
upon it.

8.7   The Fourth Antinomy: The Necessity of Nature (B480–3 and 587–95)

The Fourth Antinomy concerns the existence of an absolutely
necessary being. The thesis asserts that there is such a being that
is either in the world or is the cause of the world (see A452/B480),
but the "Proof" of the thesis argues for the stronger claim that
"Something absolutely necessary is . . . contained in the world
itself" (A454/B482). The antithesis denies that there is an absolutely
necessary being either within the world or outside it (see A453/
B481). Kant makes it clear that the world he is referring to here is
the world of sense, that is, nature.

The argument for the thesis consists of two steps, which may
be summarized as follows. First, nature "contains a series of

alterations" each of which is causally necessitated by "its condition, which precedes it in time"; but the condition cannot necessitate the alteration unless it, too, is necessitated; so "the existence of something absolutely necessary must be granted" (A452/B480). Second, whatever necessitates something in time must be in time, so "Something absolutely necessary is therefore contained in the world itself, whether this something be the whole series of alterations in the world or part of the series" (A454/B482).

The "Proof" of the antithesis also involves two steps, the first of which argues that there cannot be an absolutely necessary being within the world of sense, while the second argues that there cannot be an absolutely necessary being outside it. According to the first argument, an absolutely necessary being within the world would have to be either "a beginning in the series of alterations" or "the series itself"; but the first alternative is impossible because it "conflicts with the dynamical law of the determination of all appearances in time"—that is, with the Analogies—and the second alternative is impossible because "a series cannot be necessary if no single member of it is necessary" (A456/B482). Here it is worth recalling that (as noted in Section 5.6) Kant supports the claim that nothing in such an empirical series can be absolutely necessary in his discussion of the Third Postulate (see A226–30/B279–82). According to the second argument, there cannot be an absolutely necessary being outside the world, because it would have to begin acting at some time, so it would "belong to the sum of appearances, that is, to the world" after all (A455/B483).

Because the Fourth Antinomy is dynamical, Kant seeks to resolve it by claiming that "Both of the conflicting propositions may be true, if taken in different connections" (A560/B588). In order for this reconciliation to work, it is necessary to adjust the thesis and the antithesis so that thesis becomes *There is a necessary being, but not in nature* and the antithesis becomes *There is no necessary being in nature*. But there is still an asymmetry between them, because it turns out that we cannot know the thesis (which belongs to transcendent metaphysics) (see A565–6/B593–4), but we can know the antithesis. So Kant claims to have shown only that "the thoroughgoing contingency of all natural things . . . is quite *consistent with the optional assumption* of a necessary, though purely intelligible, condition" outside nature (A562/B590, italics added). Kant's examination of the transcendent idea of an absolutely necessary being— namely, God—is the topic of the Ideal, which we consider in the following section.

8.8 The Ideal: God (B595–619, 624–9, 632–4, 637–8, and 653–6)

The category underlying Kant's idea of God is the concept of *community*. He calls his idea of God *the Transcendental Ideal*. Embraced within the Ideal are the ideas of "an individual object which is completely determined through . . . [that] idea" (A574/ B602); of "an *ens realissimum*" (A576/604), that is, of a most fully real (or perfect) being; of "the supreme and complete material condition of the possibility of all that exists" (A576/B604); of "the *primordial being*" (A578/B606); and of "the highest reality," which is "one, simple, all-sufficient, eternal, etc." (A580/B608). How could the category of community be transformed into such a rich and comprehensive idea by being freed "from the unavoidable limitations of possible experience" (A409/B435)? Kant provides a convoluted answer to this question in section 2 of the Ideal (A571–83/B599–611).

In outline, his answer may be reconstructed as follows. Recall that the category of community expresses the logical form of disjunction, which, according to Kant, serves to present a complete or exhaustive set of alternatives (see pp.51 and 54). Freed from the limits of possible experience, this becomes the idea of a "*sum-total of all possibility*" (A573/B602). As I have expressed it here, this idea is a general concept; and general concepts—as opposed to individual things—are not fully determinate. In other words, while an individual thing may be assumed to have or lack any given property, a general concept covers only some of the properties of the possible things to which it applies and is silent about their other properties. So, if the idea *sum-total of all possibility* is indeed to embrace *all* possibilities, it must become "the concept of an individual object which is completely determined" (A574/B602) and which "contains . . . the whole store of material from which all possible predicates of things must be taken" (A575/B603). If so, this "supreme being" is no longer the *sum* of all possibility but a being that "must condition the possibility of all things as their *ground*" (A579/B607).

It may be doubted whether this account of how reason arrives at the Ideal is, as Kant claims, "natural" (A581/B609). But Kant is right to claim that the procedure involves the illegitimate substitution (or "subreption"—A583/B611) of "the *collective* unity" of the sum of all possibility for "the *distributive* unity" expressed by the category of community (A582/B610). More important at this point is Kant's insistence that we have no right to assume that the Ideal applies to a transcendent God, which is "a mere fiction" (A580/B608). For, as he claims (referring back to the Analytic), "No ... objects, besides those of the senses, can ... be given to us, and nowhere save in the context of a possible experience" (A582/610). So a transcendent God cannot be "an object *for us*" (A582/610)—that is, an object of cognition. Thus knowledge of God and the existence of God is impossible.

Kant proceeds to back this up by challenging three standard arguments for the existence of God even though this should not be necessary for the purposes of the *Critique*. The arguments, which express what Kant takes to be the only possible ways to prove the existence of God, are the ontological argument, in which the premises are drawn "from mere concepts"; the cosmological argument, which begins with "experience of existence in general"; and the "*physico-theological* proof" (Kant's name for the argument from design), which begins with "determinate experience and the specific constitution of the world of sense as thereby cognized" (A590–1/B618–19). I will give only a very brief overview of Kant's treatment of these arguments, because it contributes so little to the main line of reasoning in the *Critique*.[10] In doing this, I will consider only Kant's direct criticisms of each argument and will not discuss his arguments for the claim that "the physico-theological proof ... rests upon the cosmological proof, and the cosmological upon the ontological" (A630/B658), or the additional criticism associated with this claim.

The ontological argument is as follows. The concept of the *ens realisimum* is that of a possible being that "possesses all reality"; and since "'all reality' includes existence," it would be "self-contradictory" to reject this being (A596–7/B624–5). Kant's response draws on a point he makes in the Postulates, namely, that the categories of modality do not express properties of objects, so even a complete concept of a thing leaves it open whether the thing is possible, actual, or necessary (see A219/B266). He applies this in the Ideal by claiming that "There is already a contradiction in introducing the concept of existence ... into the concept of a thing which we profess to be thinking solely in reference to its possibility" (A597/B625). For doing so would render the proposition that God exists analytic, which is inconsistent with the fact that "all existential propositions are synthetic" (A598/B626). In short, the argument cannot work because "'*Being*' [or *existence*] is . . . not a real predicate . . . which could be added to the concept of a thing" (A598/B626). This claim about the logic of the word *exists* is now widely accepted, for one does not supplement the description of a possible thing (no matter how perfect) by adding that it exists—and one cannot ensure its existence by doing so.

Kant presents the cosmological argument in two steps. First, "If anything exists, an absolutely necessary being must also exist," and "I . . . exist," so "an absolutely necessary being exists" (A604/B632). Second, this being must be "*completely* determined through its own concept: so it must be "the *ens realissimum*," that is, a "supreme being" (A605–6/B633–4). Kant's most important direct criticisms of this argument concern the assumption underlying the first step, namely, that anything that exists is necessitated, which requires something absolutely necessary. This is a variation of the thesis of the Fourth Antinomy, so it is not surprising that his criticisms of the assumption (see A619-20/B638-9) repeat material from his response to that Antinomy—in particular, that the indefinite series of causes in nature do not justify a commitment to "a first cause . . . within the world of experience, [and] still less beyond this world in a realm into which this series can never be extended" (A610/B638).

The core of the physico-theological argument for the existence of God is that "In the world we everywhere find clear signs of an order in accordance with a determinate purpose, carried out with great wisdom," from which it is inferred that the world must have "a sublime and wise cause" (A625/B653). The core of Kant's criticism of this argument is that, to establish the conclusion, it would be necessary "to demonstrate that things in the world would not of themselves be capable of such order and harmony" (A627/B655), and this cannot be done.

Kant welcomes his conclusion that we cannot know of the existence of God, because this frees up the assumption that God exists for use as a postulate of pure practical reason in the second *Critique* (see p.133). Kant also holds that the idea of God—the Ideal—makes an important contribution toward the guidance of the understanding, which we will consider in the following section.

8.9 The Regulative Function of Ideas (B670–9, 536–7, 644–8, and 708–16)

As we have seen, Kant holds that the ideas of pure reason do not apply to objects of experience and so do not occur in judgments that express theoretical knowledge (as opposed to practical knowledge). But he still thinks that they play a significant constructive role with respect to theoretical knowledge. They do so by "positing a certain collective unity as the goal of activities of the understanding" (A644/B672). The pursuit of this goal will give the categories "that unity which they can have only if they be employed in their widest possible application" (A643/B671). So Kant claims that while "transcendental ideas never allow of any constitutive employment" with respect to objects of experience, they still "have an excellent, and indeed indispensably necessary, regulative employment" (A644/B672)—namely, to direct the understanding to pursue the goal I have mentioned. In other words, he holds that reason enjoins the understanding to apply the categories to as great a range of phenomena as possible.

Before we say more about this view, let us consider the question of how the regulative status of the ideas of reason is connected with the regulative status of the dynamical principles. Kant addresses this question as follows:

> In the Transcendental Analytic . . . we distinguished the *dynamical* principles of the understanding, as merely regulative principles of *intuition*, from the *mathematical*, which, as regards intuition, are constitutive. None the less these dynamical laws are constitutive in respect of *experience*, since they render the *concepts*, without which there can be no experience, possible *a priori*. But principles of pure reason can never be constitutive in respect of empirical *concepts*, for . . . they can never have an object *in concreto*. (A664/B692)

This may be unpacked as follows. The dynamical principles are not constitutive with respect to intuition because the possibility of intuition does not in and of itself require that these principles be satisfied. Nevertheless, the dynamical principles (which are merely regulative with respect to intuition) are constitutive with respect to experience—that is, thick experience, which involves the capacity to make objective judgments—because experience itself requires that they be satisfied. In contrast, principles of pure reason are not constitutive with respect to experience, because the possibility of experience does not in and of itself require that these principles be satisfied. But this still leaves open the possibility of their being regulative with respect to experience inasmuch as they aim it in a certain direction, namely, that of applying the categories as broadly as possible.

In the Antinomy, Kant briefly discusses the regulative use of the cosmological ideas before presenting his resolutions of the Antinomies. As he puts it, "the [cosmological] principle of reason is . . . properly only a *rule*, prescribing a regress in the series of conditions of given appearances, and forbidding it to bring the regress to a close by treating anything at which it may arrive as absolutely unconditioned" (A508–9/B536–7). With respect to experience, this is a regulative principle according to which "no empirical limit [is] to hold as absolute" (A509/B537). In other words, the principle enjoins us to continue expanding the range of phenomena which we bring within the scope of the understanding as far as possible along the four indefinite series of conditions dealt with in the Antinomy of Pure Reason.

In the Ideal, after discussing the cosmological argument for the existence of God, Kant argues that "the ideal of the supreme being is nothing but a *regulative principle* of reason which directs us to look at all connection in the world *as if* it originated from an all-sufficient necessary cause" (A619/B647). In the second part of the Appendix to the Transcendental Dialectic, he explains this by observing that it will help us progress toward "The greatest possible systematic unity" in our understanding of the world (A694/B722). In the *Critique of Judgment* (1790), the idea of treating the world as a product of God is supplemented by the idea of the purposiveness of nature, which Kant explores in Part II, where he deals with teleological (or purposive) judgment in general.

In the second part of the Appendix to the Dialectic, Kant also confirms the above account of the regulative use of the cosmological ideas (see A684–5/B712–13) and discusses the regulative use of the idea of the soul, which he does not mention in the Paralogisms. What he says is that, in investigating the self empirically, we should aim as far as possible to understand "all determinations as existing in a single subject, all powers . . . as derived from a single fundamental power, all change as belonging to the states of one and the same permanent being, and all *appearances* in space as completely different from the actions of *thought*" (A683/B711). This approach will, of course, help to ensure that we advance toward an understanding of the self that is as unitary as the evidence permits.

In the first part of the Appendix to the Transcendental Dialectic, Kant discusses the regulative function of the ideas of pure reason in general terms. This function is to "direct the understanding beyond every given experience . . . and thereby to secure its greatest possible extension" (A645/B673). In its regulative use, "what is peculiarly distinctive of reason . . . is that it prescribes and seeks to achieve . . . [the] *systematisation* [of experience], that is, to exhibit the connection of its parts in conformity with a single principle" (A645/B673). So reason urges us not merely to expand the range of phenomena to which we apply our concepts of understanding but also to seek unity in diversity through the application of concepts and principles of the understanding. To be sure, reason cannot establish that such unity must exist (see A649/B677), so this principle is methodological rather than substantive. But, from the perspective of the twenty-first century, it is evident that the principle has played an important role in the systematic development of modern science.

In claiming that principles of reason are regulative rather than constitutive with respect to the understanding, Kant is recognizing that human cognition—our capacity to know—need not be exercised as broadly and systematically as possible in order to be the capacity that it is. But there is something in human beings that drives some of them to try to apply their cognitive powers in this way some of the time. Kant ascribes this propensity to reason. In doing so, he is claiming that it has the same source as the drive toward the illusions of transcendent metaphysics (which we are, however, capable of resisting). He is also implying that the propensity has the same source as our capacity for normative reasoning, which depends upon ideas of reason. So it is not surprising that in the *Grounding for the Metaphysics of Morals*—which was published in 1785, two years before the second edition of the *Critique of Pure Reason*—Kant expresses a commitment to the unity of practical and theoretical reason:

> [T]here must . . . be the possibility . . . of showing the unity of
> practical and speculative reason in a common principle; for in
> the final analysis there can be only one and the same reason,
> which must be differentiated solely in its application. (4:391)

But Kant's attempt to establish the unity of practical and theoretical
reason must await the *Critique of Practical Reason*, where he also
argues that the practical application of pure reason takes priority
over its speculative application (see 5:119–21).

9

Taking Stock

This short final chapter consists of two sections. The first provides an overview of my picture of Kant's position by presenting my considered accounts of his transcendental idealism—which is the unifying theme of the *Critique of Pure Reason*—and his talk about things in themselves. The second is a brief discussion of Kant's achievement in this remarkable work.

9.1 Transcendental Idealism and Things in Themselves (B274–9 and 288–94)

In philosophy, *idealism* in the broadest sense is the view that the mind—the locus of ideas—is in some way fundamental. There are several varieties of idealism. In the *Critique*, Kant pays special attention to his own transcendental idealism and two other important types of idealism that he utterly rejects. One of these is "the *problematic* idealism of Descartes," which "declares the existence of objects in space outside us to be . . . doubtful and indemonstrable" (B274).[1] The other is "the *dogmatic* idealism of Berkeley," which "declares the existence of objects in space outside us . . . to be false and impossible" (B274).[2] So Descartes holds that knowledge of oneself and the contents of one's own mind—one's ideas—are fundamental, and that any knowledge we may have of other things depends upon this knowledge and is subject to doubt. And Berkeley holds that ordinary objects are not independent substances outside us but are constituted by ideas. Kant uses the phrase "*material* idealism" to cover both these positions (B274), and he sometimes calls his transcendental idealism "*formal* idealism" to emphasize that it is distinct from material idealism (A491/B519 fn., see also *Prolegomena* 4:337).

Kant seeks to undermine material idealism in the Refutation of Idealism, a short section that he added to the second edition of the *Critique* in the middle of the Postulates (see B274–9). He attempts to do this by arguing for the thesis that "*The mere, but empirically determined, consciousness of my own existence proves the existence of objects in space outside me*" (B275). The core of Kant's "Proof" of the theorem is that it follows from two facts: first, that "I am conscious of my own existence as determined in time"—which is an empirical consciousness that goes beyond what is expressed by the "I think" of pure apperception—and, second, that "the determination of my existence in time is possible only through the existence of actual things which I perceive outside me" (B275–6).[3] It is obvious that this draws on the Analogies and the Postulates.

Indeed, there are a number of places in addition to the Refutation of Idealism where Kant insists on the priority of outer cognition, including the Paralogisms in A (see A381–2), the Preface in B (see the footnote on Bxxxix–xli), and the General Note on the System of Principles, which he added after the Postulates in the B edition (see B288–94). Kant opens this important passage by identifying "a very noteworthy fact," namely, "That the possibility of a thing cannot be determined from the category alone, and that in order to exhibit the objective reality of the pure concept of the understanding we must always have an intuition" (B288). A little later, he goes on to say this:

> [I]t is an even more noteworthy fact that in order to understand the possibility of things in conformity with the categories, and so to establish the *objective reality* of the latter, we need, not merely intuitions, but intuitions that are in all cases *outer intuitions*. (B291)

Kant defends this claim by noting that we cannot apply the relational categories to objects without outer sense. More specifically, it is only through outer sense that we are able to "obtain something *permanent* in intuition corresponding to the concept of *substance*," to "exhibit alteration as the intuition corresponding to the concept of *causality*," and to have intuitions that display "the possibility of the category of *community*" (B291–2). These claims are well illustrated by Kant's arguments in support of the Analogies and the Second Postulate, which depend on both the spatiality of intuitions of outer sense and the relative stability and constancy of these intuitions to ground our access to an objective spatio-temporal system. In contrast, as he suggests in the Transcendental Deduction, my intuitions of inner sense are so "many-coloured and diverse" that they cannot in themselves exhibit unity (B134). So it is not surprising that Kant holds that a category "can be exhibited only in outer intuition, and that only through the mediation of outer intuition can it be applied also to inner sense" (B293). What he has in mind here is that we can understand intuitions of inner sense as occurring in objective time and thus as falling under categories only by connecting these intuitions with outer appearances as required by the Analogies.

Kant rejects material idealism unequivocally for these reasons. Yet some things he says about transcendental idealism seem perilously close to Berkeley's idealism—but with inaccessible things in themselves tacked on gratuitously behind appearances. This applies in particular to Kant's repeated remark that appearances (which includes everything in nature) are mere presentations (see, for example, A104, A369, A490–1/B518–19, A492/B520), which clearly suggests that ordinary objects are mind-dependent. But in Chapter 3, I argued in some detail against this interpretation of Kantian appearances and the subjectivist interpretation of Kant's account of space and time that goes along with it. I have accordingly been interpreting appearances as independent objects insofar as they are accessible to our cognition. Kant's rejection of Berkeley's idealism helps to support this approach.

But what, then, does Kant's transcendental idealism amount to? Neither the *Critique* nor the *Prolegomena* contains a systematic, chapter-length exposition of the doctrine that answers this question. The reason, I think, is that transcendental idealism is best understood as embracing and unifying the most central claims of the *Critique of Pure Reason* as a whole.[4] This claim is not surprising if we go back to basics and ask what "transcendental idealism" means. As idealism, it must imply that the mind is in some way fundamental. As transcendental, it must be concerned with how synthetic *a priori* cognition is possible (see Section 2.5). These two aspects of transcendental idealism come together in Kant's

Copernican Hypothesis. For the Copernican Hypothesis is idealistic inasmuch as its claim that "objects must conform to our cognition" (Bxvi) implies that the mind is in a certain way fundamental. And it is transcendental inasmuch as this claim is meant to explain how synthetic *a priori* knowledge is possible.

But this still does not reveal exactly how, according to Kant, the mind is fundamental. It cannot be that he holds that the mind is fundamental in the sense that the existence of objects of cognition depends upon it, for this is material idealism. Moreover, he explicitly claims that an *a priori* presentation "does not produce the object in so far as *existence* is concerned" (A92/B125)—and, as I have argued, the assumption that it does cannot accommodate Kant's view that, although objects must conform to our cognitions insofar as we can have *a priori* knowledge of them, our cognitions must conform to these same objects insofar as we can have *a posteriori* knowledge of them. The alternative account which I have advanced and unpacked in this book is that Kant holds that the mind is fundamental in the sense that independent objects must conform to the *a priori* forms of sensibility and understanding *in order to be possible objects of experience* about which we can have knowledge—including, in particular, empirical knowledge. This account makes good sense of Kant's description of transcendental idealism as formal idealism.

According to this account, things in themselves do not play a significant part in Kant's transcendental idealism. This should not be surprising given Kant's insistence that "in experience no question is ever asked in regard to [the thing in itself]" (A30/B45). What, then, is the function of Kant's talk about things in themselves in the *Critique of Pure Reason*? The notion of things in themselves (or noumena) does not make a positive contribution to Kant's constructive account of cognition as I have explained it. But it does have the negative function of helping Kant explain the scope and limits of cognition by referring whatever lies beyond these limits to things in themselves. That this is correct is evident from Kant's observation that "The concept of a noumenon is a . . . merely *limiting concept*, the function of which is to curb the pretensions of sensibility" (A255/B310–11), as well as by his later remark that "if the concept of noumenon is taken in a merely problematic sense, it is not only admissible, but *as setting limits to sensibility* likewise indispensable" (A256/B311, italics added).[5]

TAKING STOCK163

It is true that the claim that things in themselves do not play a constructive role in Kant's account of cognition is at odds with his suggestion in the Preface that we must posit things in themselves because "otherwise we should be landed in the absurd conclusion that there can be appearance without anything that appears" (Bxxvi–xxvii). But this unfortunate remark fails to address the fact that it is appearances, or objects of experience, that appear to us through intuition, not transcendent objects. Perhaps Kant should not have called objects in nature *appearances*, because this is misleading, but appearances as he understands them do not presuppose things in themselves.

Kant's most important positive applications of the notion of things in themselves occur in the Dialectic, where he appeals to them to accommodate the possibility of freedom, God, and the immortality of the soul. At the same time, Kant insists that we cannot cognize, let alone know, that we are free, that God exists, or that the soul is immortal, even though he holds that these claims are required as postulates of practical reason. This is convincing only in the case of freedom, which is presupposed by morality. And, as we saw in connection with the Third Antinomy, it is necessary to distinguish the "noumenal" perspective of normative reasoning from the phenomenal perspective of our cognition about what is the case in order to accommodate the possibility of freedom. But, as I suggested in Section 8.6, it is not necessary to posit things in themselves in order to draw this distinction, and attributing causes from freedom to things in themselves does not explain how freedom of action is possible.

Be that as it may, the core of Kant's transcendental idealism is the claim that the form of our cognition determines what kinds of things are possible objects of knowledge, including empirical knowledge.[6] Kant elaborates and defends this claim over the course of the *Critique of Pure Reason*. In the Aesthetic he argues that objects must be spatio-temporal if it is to be possible for us to perceive them. In the Analytic he argues that the categories and fundamental principles must apply to them if it is to be possible for us to make objective judgments and have knowledge about them. In the Dialectic he argues that, given these conditions, we cannot have knowledge that transcends the limits of possible experience.

If successful, Kant's reasoning shows that any world about which we could have experience and knowledge must be a unitary spatio-temporal world of substance and substances in which events and processes are part of a pervasively interconnected causal system (see Section 1.1). Some might object that Kant does not show that these basic structural features of our world are, so to speak, absolutely necessary, but only, at best, that they are necessary relative to the forms of our cognition. I believe that this is indeed the case, but I also hold that it gives us the strongest necessity other than logical necessity that we could appreciate or reasonably aspire to. Not even Kant can get beyond the limits of human cognitive powers or stand outside the human point of view.

9.2 Kant's Achievement

No well-considered assessment of Kant's achievement in the *Critique of Pure Reason* should depend upon a particular interpretation of this elusive work—or on the unfortunate fact that it is open to so many conflicting interpretations. To appreciate Kant's achievement, we must consider not only his indisputable substantial contributions to philosophy but also the new possibilities that he opened up by the introduction of new conceptual resources, new questions and problems, new ways of tackling problems, and other changes in perspective and approach. In this light, Kant's *Critique of Pure Reason* qualifies as one of the most revolutionary works in the history of philosophy, and perhaps the most revolutionary since the time of Plato and Aristotle. I will mention only a few considerations that illustrate and help to support this claim.

Among the most significant ways in which Kant helped to advance philosophy was by expanding and enriching its conceptual and methodological repertoire. His most important contributions to the conceptual resources of philosophy include the analytic/synthetic distinction and the notions of *synthetic a priori knowledge, a metaphysics of experience, the productive imagination,* and *synthesis*—all of which opened up novel philosophical possibilities. At the same time, Kant set new aspirational standards for the explication of important concepts and distinctions. For, even though his own writing is often unclear, he struggles far more than his predecessors in modern philosophy to elucidate his most important concepts and distinctions and to draw out the relationships between them.

Kant also enriched the methodological resources of philosophy by his exceptional commitment to digging up the underlying presuppositions of significant general propositions about human capacities that are or may be taken for granted. Such a commitment can lead to a productive shift in perspective and background assumptions—a shift which is most dramatically exemplified in the *Critique of Pure Reason* by Kant's Copernican Hypothesis. Kant's relentless pursuit of presuppositions is also manifest in one of his most crucial contributions to the advancement of philosophy. What I have in mind is his introduction of an important new type of question: the characteristically Kantian question of how something is possible.

Kant applies this question to things that are taken to be significant to human beings and are widely assumed to be actual. The question allows him—and us—to break through the standoff between skeptics, who doubt or deny the supposed fact on the ground that it cannot be established on the basis of established principles, and dogmatists, who embrace the supposed fact as a principle merely because they feel it cannot be questioned. Kant's *how-possible* question does not succumb either to the skeptical dogma that whatever is open to any possible doubt must be sealed off and set aside, or to the dogmatic enthusiasm that helps itself to whatever it feels it needs. By allowing that the supposed fact might be the case and seeking an explanation of its possibility, Kant's question requires a much deeper, critical investigation into the supposed fact's place in and contributions to human experience. And this investigation itself could either strengthen or undermine its claim to our endorsement.

It is worth adding here that the most important *how-possible* question raised by the *Critique of Pure Reason* may not be the one to which Kant gives most prominence, namely, *How is synthetic a priori knowledge possible?* As I see it, the most important how-possible question raised by the *Critique* is, rather, the more modest question *How is human empirical knowledge possible?* This question is more modest because it is much easier to grant that we have empirical knowledge than to grant that we have synthetic *a priori* knowledge. And it is pivotal, because Kant's defense of synthetic *a priori* knowledge depends upon his arguments for the claim that his fundamental synthetic *a priori* principles and the *a priori* concepts which they involve are presupposed by empirical knowledge and are required to explain how it is possible.

Finally, I will mention just a sprinkling of the many substantial ways in which Kant contributed to the development of philosophy. He moved beyond the skeptical perspective which so dominated the work of Descartes and the British Empiricists. He broke down the conflict between Rationalism and Empiricism and found enlightening ways of exploiting their insights to develop a deeply original new perspective. He recognized the achievements of natural science and the importance of accommodating and respecting these achievements in philosophy. And he provided reasons for thinking that there can be no science of ethics and freedom, and that transcendent metaphysics is forever doomed.

Kant's *Critique of Pure Reason* has changed the landscapes and horizons of philosophy. It is a formidable achievement that is unmatched in philosophy in the modern era.

NOTES

Bibliographical details of secondary sources cited in these notes appear in the Bibliography. In the case of major historical works, alternative versions are almost always available.

Preface

1 See Paul Guyer, *Kant and the Claims of Knowledge*, 336.

Chapter 1

1 Wilfrid Sellars (1912–89), "Philosophy and the Scientific Image of Man," in his *Science, Perception and Reality*, 1. Acknowledgment: I thank the Ridgeview Publishing Company of Atascadero, California, for permission to use this quotation as an epigraph.

2 Relevant issues are discussed in Locke's *An Essay Concerning Human Understanding* (1689) and Reid's *Essays on the Intellectual Powers of Man* (1785).

3 Much of Leibniz's most significant philosophical work is scattered through his numerous shorter papers and correspondence. Notable works relevant to the issues mentioned here include the "Discourse on Metaphysics" (1686), Leibniz's correspondence with Arnauld (1686–7), and the "Monadology" (1714), his popular summary of his philosophical position. Translations of all three appear in G. W. Leibniz, *Philosophical Texts*, edited by Woolhouse and Franks.

4 Hume discusses issues related to those mentioned in Book I of *A Treatise on Human Nature* (1738). Page references below are to the Selby-Bigge version (see Bibliography).

5 James uses the phrase "One Great Blooming, Buzzing Confusion" for what he takes to be a baby's response to external stimuli in *The Principles of Psychology* (1890), 462.

6 This position is most famously associated with Georg Wilhelm Friederich Hegel (1770–1831), whose most important works include *The Phenomenology of Spirit* (1807) and *The Science of Logic* (1812–16).

7 Translator's Preface, Kemp Smith translation of the *Critique of Pure Reason*, 2007 edition, xxiv. (For bibliographical details, see p. xv.)

Chapter 2

1 The phrase "the metaphysics of experience" is adapted from the title H. J. Paton's important study, *Kant's Metaphysic of Experience*.

2 For more information, see p.xvi.

3 The word here translated as *presentation*, namely, *Vorstellung*, is rendered as *representation* in many translations. For more information, see pp.xvi–xvii.

4 C. I. Lewis, *Mind and the World Order*, 30, 54. In applying Lewis's distinction to the *Critique of Pure Reason*, I follow James Van Cleve, *Problems from Kant*, 73–4.

5 Quine's challenge to these distinctions appears most dramatically in "Two Dogmas of Empiricism." The analytic/synthetic distinction is defended against Quine's challenge in H. P. Grice and P. F. Strawson, "In Defense of a Dogma."

6 For a discussion of some questions concerning the analytic/synthetic distinction and other aspects of the introduction to the *Critique of Pure Reason*, see R. Lanier Anderson, "The Introduction to the *Critique*: Framing the Question."

7 Here are some examples of such challenges. In *The Foundations of Arithmetic* (1884), 17ᶜ–21ᵉ, Gottlob Frege (1848–1925), the founder of modern logic and a towering figure in the philosophy of mathematics, argues that the truths of arithmetic are analytic but accepts that the truths of geometry are synthetic *a priori*. In his 1921 address to the Prussian Academy of Sciences, Albert Einstein (1879–1955) argues without specifically mentioning Kant that "as far as the laws of mathematics refer to reality, they are not certain; and as far as they are certain, they do not refer to reality" ("Geometry and Experience," 233). Since claims that "refer to reality" are synthetic and those that are "certain" are necessary and *a priori*, this rules out synthetic *a priori* truths in geometry. In *Language, Truth and Logic*, 79–87, A. J. Ayer (1910–89), the champion of logical positivism in Britain, argues that all truths of mathematics are analytic.

8 See James Van Cleve, *Problems From Kant*, 23–4.

Chapter 3

1 "§1," "§2," etc.: Kant inserted this very useful series of section numbers—which cut across other subdivisions of the *Critique*—in the B edition between B33 and B169. These section numbers are widely used to refer to material covered in these pages.

2 The view that Kantian appearances are to be understood as mind-dependent objects is advanced in, for example, Wilfrid Sellars *Science and Metaphysics* (see Chapter II), Richard Aquila, *Representational Mind* (see especially Chapter 4), and James Van Cleve, *Problems from Kant* (see especially 8–12). The view that appearances are objects that are largely independent of our intuitions is supported in great detail but in very different ways in, for example, Henry Allison, *Kant's Transcendental Idealism*, Rae Langton, *Kantian Humility*, and Lucy Allais, *Manifest Reality*.

3 This conception of ideas was criticized by Reid in *Essays on the Intellectual Powers of Man*, especially Essay II, Chapter 14 ("Reflections on the Common Theory of Ideas").

4 Much later Kant introduces the further notion of a *formal intuition*, which goes beyond the notion of the *form of intuition* (see Section 6.4).

5 For a careful attempt to explain how time attaches to outer sense, see Ralf Bader, "Inner Sense and Time."

6 This applies to, for example, P. F. Strawson, *The Bounds of Sense*, 47–62, Jonathan Bennett, *Kant's Analytic*, 61–7, and Henry E. Allison, *Kant's Transcendental Idealism*, 97–137.

7 The problem is clearly recognized by Sellars in *Science and Metaphysics*, Chapter I, but it seems to me that Sellars's response to this "absurdity" (30) depends upon far too literalistic an interpretation of Kant.

8 See, for example, Gottlob Frege, *The Foundations of Arithmetic*, 21e.

Chapter 4

1 John McDowell, *Mind and World*, especially 3–23, 46–65, and 162–74. McDowell attributes the view that the contents of intuitions are conceptual to Kant without arguing in detail that it is Kant's view. Most of his discussion of the relationship between intuitions and concepts is aimed, rather, at supporting the view in its own right. The

claim that Kant is committed to the view is opposed by, for example, Allais in *Manifest Reality*, 145–75.

2   John McDowell, *Mind and World*, 52.

3   John McDowell, "Avoiding the Myth of the Given," 266.

4   One of the most notable exceptions is Béatrice Longuenesse, who depends upon the Metaphysical Deduction in *Kant and the Capacity to Judge*.

5   For a careful attempt to explain Kant's Table of Judgments, see Michael Wolff, "How Precise Is Kant's Table of Judgments?"

Chapter 5

1   The third chapter of the Analytic of Principles—The Ground of the Distinction of all Objects in General into Phenomena and Noumena— does not deal with anything essentially new but unpacks Kant's concepts of *phenomenon* and *noumenon* and helps to clarify his earlier reasoning. Although I do not discuss this chapter in its own right, I cite it and draw on it in a number of places.

2   Such an interpretation is advanced by, for example, Paul Guyer in *Kant and the Claims of Knowledge*—see especially 148.

3   In *Categories of the Temporal*, Sebastian Rödl supports the thesis that if our thought depends upon objects given by intuition, then it must be temporal and must apply both to things that are in time and to things that occur over time. Hence there must be "categories of the temporal." In the *Critique of Pure Reason*, these are the relational categories, the temporality of which is on full display in Analogies of Experience. Rödl discusses the First Analogy on 113–27 (where he also criticizes epistemological interpretations of the Analogies) and the Second Analogy on 180–6.

4   In "Epistemic Normativity in Kant's 'Second Analogy'," James Hutton argues that the necessity of the subjective order of appearances is a matter of epistemic normativity. I see it, rather, as a logical consequence of all the applicable factors, including the nature of causality. Although this gives rise to epistemic normativity, it also goes deeper than that.

5   David Hume, *Treatise of Human Nature*, 76 (Book I, Part III, Section II: "Of Probability; and of the Idea of Cause and Effect").

6   This includes both Pluhar and Guyer and Wood.

7 The speed of light was first measured by the Danish astronomer Ole Christensen Rømer (1644–1710) in 1676, almost a century before the publication of the first edition of the *Critique* in 1771.

8 For a much more detailed discussion of the Postulates, see Ian Blecher, "Kant's Principles of Modality."

Chapter 6

1 David Hume makes a similar point about "bodies" in *A Treatise of Human Nature*, 187–9 (Book I, Part IV, Section II: "Of Skepticism with Regard to the Senses").

2 Jonathan Bennett, *Kant's Analytic*, 100.

3 The seminal work on the two stages of the Deduction in B is Dieter Henrich, "The Proof-Structure of Kant's Transcendental Deduction."

4 This section runs from B124 to B129. The heading "§14" was accidentally omitted from the B edition of the *Critique*, but it was added in the third edition. It is included in the Kemp Smith and Pluhar translations but not in the Guyer and Wood translation.

5 David Hume, *A Treatise of Human Nature*, 252 (Book I, Part IV, Section VI: "Of Personal Identity").

6 For a careful discussion of some different interpretations of the transcendental unity of apperception, see Patricia Kitcher, "The Critical and 'Empty' Representation 'I Think.'"

7 P. F. Strawson, *The Bounds of Sense*, 92–3.

8 There are several other accounts of the two stages of the Deduction in B. Here are three examples. In "The Proof-Structure of the Transcendental Deduction," Henrich claims that the first stage argues that "intuitions are subject to the categories *insofar* as they . . . already possess unity" (645), while the second stage overcomes this restriction and argues that "the categories are valid for *all* objects of our senses" (646). In *Transcendental Idealism*, Allison claims that the first stage asserts "the necessity of the categories . . . with respect to objects of intuition in general" (including non-human intuition), while the second stage "argues for the necessity of the categories with respect to human sensibility and its object" (160). In *Kant's Deduction from Apperception*, Dennis Schulting claims that in the first stage Kant aims to show that "the categories . . . are deducible or derivable from . . . the principle

of apperception" (1)—which is to say that that all the categories are implicit in the "I think" of apperception (see, for example, 34, 71, 123)—while in the second stage Kant aims to show that "necessarily, perceptions are subject to the categories if and only if they are to contribute to knowledge" (19).

9 Yet some commentators claim that in §26 Kant is trying to explain the spatio-temporal form of intuitions. See, for example, Henry E. Allison, *Kant's Transcendental Idealism*, 185–97.

10 This footnote has given rise to considerable discussion in the scholarly literature. For an overview of relevant contributions, see Christian Onof and Dennis Schulting, "Space as Form of Intuition and as Formal Intuition."

11 Béatrice Longuenesse, *Kant and the Capacity to Judge*. The following quotations are from pages 64 and 12 respectively.

12 This view is developed and defended by T. A. Pendlebury in "The Shape of the Kantian Mind."

13 It might be thought that this harmony could be merely a Leibnizian pre-established harmony, but Kant rejects such an account of the necessary application of the categories (see B166–8). Moreover, as early as 1755 Kant makes it clear that he thinks that pre-established harmony is not genuine harmony, which requires reciprocal dependency: "There exists a universal *harmony* of things. Nonetheless, this does not give rise to the well-known Leibnizian *pre-established harmony*, which is properly speaking *agreement* between substance, not their *reciprocal dependency* on each other." (*New Elucidation of the First Principles of Metaphysical Cognition*, I:415, italics changed.)

14 C. I. Lewis, *Mind and the World Order*, 221.

15 The seminal work is H. Wimmer and I. Perner, "Beliefs about Beliefs."

16 Donald Davidson, *Subjective, Intersubjective, Objective*, especially essay 7, "Rational Animals." Although I draw on Davidson here, I reject his view that in order to have beliefs, a being must have the concept of belief and thus be able to recognize the possibility that it is in error. I see this as a requirement of judgment and rationality but not of mere belief. Thus, unlike Davidson, I am free to claim that nonlinguistic animals can have beliefs.

17 Lewis White Beck, "Did the Sage of Königsberg Have No Dreams?" 51. The following quotation is from page 53.

Chapter 7

1 The core of the position advanced in this chapter is adapted from Michael Pendlebury, "Making Sense of Kant's Schematism."
2 In the Kemp Smith translation, this phrase appears as if it is on A143 because of an error in the marginal pagination.
3 A detailed defense of an interpretation of this type appears in Paul Guyer, *Kant and the Claims of Knowledge*, 157–75.
4 For an interesting explanation of the significance of Kant's description of schematism as an art, see Samantha Matherne, "Kant and the Art of Schematism."

Chapter 8

1 For an extended study of this aspect of the Dialectic, see Marcus Willaschek, *Kant on the Sources of Metaphysics*.
2 The features of the "I" of apperception reviewed in this paragraph suggest that this "I" is, as Alexandra Newton argues in "Kant and the Transparency of Mind," opaque.
3 Drawing extensively on Kant's earlier and later works, Karl Ameriks argues that in the Paralogisms Kant is, nevertheless, committed to the view that we understand ourselves as a kind of substance that is not in space or time. See Ameriks, *Kant's Theory of Mind*, especially 64–73.
4 *Grounding for the Metaphysics of Morals* (1785) and *The Metaphysics of Morals* (1797).
5 See, for example, P. F. Strawson, *The Bounds of Sense*, 176–83 (on the First Antinomy) and Henry E. Allison, *Kant's Transcendental Idealism*, 366–74 (on the First Antinomy) and 374–84 (on the Third Antinomy). For a more sympathetic view of the arguments, see Allen W. Wood, "The Antimomies of Pure Reason," 249–57.
6 See, for example, Paul Guyer, *Kant and the Claims of Knowledge* and James Van Cleve, *Problems from Kant*.
7 See, for example, Henry E. Allison, *Kant's Transcendental Idealism* and Lucy Allais, *Manifest Reality*. Allen Wood argues that the conflict between the two worlds and the two aspects accounts cannot be resolved on textual grounds in *Kant*, 63–76.
8 This is widely accepted in contemporary normative theory, where it is common ground between several competing meta-normative theories,

including non-naturalistic realism and expressivism. The most notable
exception is naturalistic realism. For accounts of these and other
positions, see, for example, Tristram McPherson and David Plunkett
(eds.), *The Routledge Handbook of Metaethics*.

9 Henry E. Allison, *Kant's Groundwork for the Metaphysics of Morals*,
354. Allison nevertheless recognizes that Kant more often uses
"overtly metaphysical language" in presenting his account of freedom
(354) but argues in support of a non-metaphysical interpretation (see
348–54).

10 For detailed accounts of Kant's treatment of the ontological and
cosmological arguments, see Ian Proops, "Kant on the Ontological
Argument" and "Kant on the Cosmological Argument."

Chapter 9

1 René Descartes (1596–1650) advances his position in *Meditations
on First Philosophy* (1641) and *The Principles of Philosophy* (1644).
Both appear in *The Philosophical Writings of Descartes* translated by
Cottingham et al.

2 George Berkeley (1685–1753) advances his idealism in *A Treatise
on the Principles of Human Knowledge* (1710) and *Three Dialogues
between Hylas and Philonous* (1713).

3 For a careful exposition of the details of the argument, see Ralf Bader,
"The Refutation of Idealism."

4 Here I concur with Allison in rejecting what he calls "the separability
thesis," according to which Kant's transcendental idealism can be
separated from his other important views and evaluated separately
(see *Kant's Transcendental Idealism*, xiv, 6–11). The following account
of transcendental idealism is similar to Allison's in some ways but
differs from it inasmuch as Allison identifies appearances with things
in themselves while I judge that things in themselves do not play an
essential part in transcendental idealism.

5 The "concept of noumenon . . . taken in a merely problematic sense"
is equivalent to that of a thing in itself and stands in contrast with the
concept of a noumenon as the object of a divine intellect.

6 For another objectivist account of Kant's transcendental idealism,
see Justin Shaddock, "Kant's Transcendental Idealism and his
Transcendental Deduction," especially 272–5.

BIBLIOGRAPHY

Allais, Lucy. *Manifest Reality: Kant's Idealism and his Realism*. Oxford: Oxford University Press, 2015.

Allison, Henry E. *Kant's Transcendental Idealism: An Interpretation and Defense*. 1983. Revised and Enlarged Edition. New Haven, CT: Yale University Press, 2004.

Allison, Henry E. *Kant's Groundwork for the Metaphysics of Morals: A Commentary*. Oxford: Oxford University Press, 2011.

Ameriks, Karl. *Kant's Theory of Mind: An Analysis of the Paralogisms of Pure Reason*. 1982. Second Edition. Oxford: Oxford University Press, 2000.

Anderson, R. Lanier. "The Introduction to the Critique: Framing the Question." In *The Cambridge Companion to Kant's Critique of Pure Reason*, edited by Paul Guyer, 75–92. Cambridge: Cambridge University Press, 2010.

Aquila, Richard. *Representational Mind: A Study of Kant's Theory of Knowledge*. Bloomington, IN: Indiana University Press, 1983.

Ayer A. J., *Language, Truth and Logic*. 1936. Second Edition. London: Victor Gollanz, 1946.

Bader, Ralf. "Inner Sense and Time." In *Kant and the Philosophy of Mind: Perception, Reason and the Self*, edited by Anil Gomes and Andrew Stephenson, 124–37. Oxford: Oxford University Press, 2017.

Bader, Ralf. "The Refutation of Idealism." In *Kant's Critique of Pure Reason: A Critical Guide*, edited by James R. O'Shea, 205–22. Cambridge: Cambridge University Press, 2017.

Beck, Lewis White. "Did the Sage of Königsberg Have No Dreams?" In *Essays on Kant and Hume*, edited by Lewis White Beck, 38–60. New Haven, CT: Yale University Press, 1978.

Bennett, Jonathan. *Kant's Analytic*. Cambridge: Cambridge University Press, 1966.

Berkeley, George. *Three Dialogues Between Hylas and Philonous*. 1713. Edited by Robert M. Adams. Indianapolis: Hackett Publishing Company, 1979.

Berkeley, George. *A Treatise Concerning the Principles of Human Knowledge*. 1710. Edited by Kenneth Winkler. Indianapolis: Hackett Publishing Company, 1985.

Blecher, Ian. "Kant's Principles of Modality." *European Journal of Philosophy* 26 (2018): 932–44.

Davidson, Donald. *Subjective, Intersubjective, Objective.* Oxford: Oxford University Press, 2001.

Descartes, René. *The Philosophical Writings of Descartes.* 2 vols. Translated by John Cottingham, Robert Stoothoff, and Dugald Murdoch. Cambridge: Cambridge University Press, 1985.

Einstein, Albert. "Geometry and Experience." 1921. Translated by Sonja Bargmann. In *Ideas and Opinions*, edited by Albert Einstein, 232–46. New York: Crown Publishers, 1982.

Frege, Gottlob. *The Foundations of Arithmetic: A Logico-Mathematical Inquiry into the Concept of Number.* 1884. Translated by J. L. Austin. Second Edition. Oxford: Blackwell, 1953.

Grice, H. P. and P. F. Strawson "In Defense of a Dogma." *Philosophical Review* 65 (1956): 141–58.

Guyer, Paul. *Kant and the Claims of Knowledge.* Cambridge: Cambridge University Press, 1987.

Hegel, Georg Wilhelm Friedrich. *The Phenomenology of Spirit.* 1807. Translated by Terry Pinkard. Cambridge: Cambridge University Press, 2018.

Hegel, Georg Wilhelm Friedrich. *The Science of Logic.* 1812–16. Translated by George di Giovanni. Cambridge: Cambridge University Press, 2010.

Henrich, Dieter. "The Proof-Structure of Kant's Transcendental Deduction." *The Review of Metaphysics* 22 (1969): 640–59.

Hume, David. *A Treatise of Human Nature.* 1738. Second Selby-Bigge Edition, edited by P. H. Nidditch. Oxford: Oxford University Press, 1978.

Hutton, James. "Epistemic Normativity in Kant's 'Analogy'." *European Journal of Philosophy* 27 (2019): 593–609.

James, William. *The Principles of Psychology.* 1890. Cambridge, MA: Harvard University Press, 1981.

Kitcher, Patricia. "The Critical and 'Empty' Representation 'I Think'." In *Kant's Critique of Pure Reason: A Critical Guide*, edited by James. R. O'Shea, 140–62. Cambridge: Cambridge University Press, 2017.

Langton, Rae. *Kantian Humility: Our Ignorance of Things in Themselves.* Oxford: Oxford University Press, 1998.

Leibniz, Gottfried Wilhelm. *Philosophical Texts.* Edited by R. S. Woolhouse and Richard Francks. Oxford: Oxford University Press, 1998.

Lewis, Clarence Irving. *Mind and the World Order.* New York: Scribners, 1929.

Locke, John. *An Essay Concerning Human Understanding.* 1689. Edited by P. H. Nidditch. Oxford: Oxford University Press, 1975.

Longuenesse, Béatrice. *Kant and the Capacity to Judge: Sensibility and Discursivity in the Transcendental Analytic of the Critique of Pure Reason*. Translated from the French by Charles T. Wolfe. Princeton, NJ: Princeton University Press, 1998.

Matherne, Samantha. "Kant and the Art of Schematism." *Kantian Review* 19 (2014): 181–205.

McDowell, John. *Mind and World*. Cambridge, MA: Harvard University Press, 1994.

McDowell, John. "Avoiding the Myth of the Given." In *Having the World in View: Essays on Hegel, Sellars and Kant*, edited by John McDowell, 256–72. Cambridge, MA: Harvard University Press, 2009.

McPherson, Tristram and David Plunkett (eds.). *The Routledge Handbook of Metaethics*. Abingdon, Oxfordshire: Routledge, 2018.

Newton, Alexandra M. "Kant and the Transparency of Mind." *Canadian Journal of Philosophy* 49 (2019): 890–915.

Onof, Christian and Dennis Schulting. "Space as Form of Intuition and as Formal Intuition: On the Note to B160 in Kant's *Critique of Pure Reason*." *Philosophical Review* 124 (2015): 1–58.

Paton, H. J. *Kant's Metaphysic of Experience: A Commentary on the First Half of the Kritik der reinen Vernunft*. 2 vols. Second Edition. London: Macmillan, 1951.

Pendlebury, Michael. "Making Sense of Kant's Schematism." *Philosophy and Phenomenological Research* 55 (1995): 777–97.

Pendlebury, T. A. "The Shape of the Kantian Mind." *Philosophy and Phenomenological Research*, advance online publication (2021): https://doi.org/10.1111/phpr.12767.

Proops, Ian. "Kant on the Cosmological Argument." *Philosophers Imprint*, 14 (2014), 1–21.

Proops, Ian. "Kant on the Ontological Argument." *Noûs* 49 (2015): 1–27.

Quine, W. V. O. "Two Dogmas of Empiricism." In *From a Logical Point of View*, edited by W. V. O. Quine, 20–46. Cambridge, MA: Harvard University Press, 1953.

Reid, Thomas. *Essays on the Intellectual Powers of Man*. 1785. Cambridge: Cambridge University Press, 2011.

Rödl, Sebastian. *Categories of the Temporal: An Inquiry into the Forms of the Finite Intellect*. Translated by Sibylle Salewski. Cambridge, MA: Harvard University Press, 2012.

Schulting, Dennis. *Kant's Deduction from Apperception: An Essay on the Transcendental Deduction of the Categories*. 2012. Second Revised Edition. Berlin: Walter de Gruyter, 2020.

Sellars, Wilfrid. "Philosophy and the Scientific Image of Man." In *Science, Perception and Reality*, edited by Wilfried Sellars, 1–40. 1963. Atascadero, CA: Ridgeview Publishing Company, 1991.

Sellars, Wilfrid. *Science and Metaphysics: Variations on Kantian Themes*.
    1967. Atascadero, CA: Ridgeview Publishing Company, 1992.
Shaddock, Justin B. "Kant's Transcendental Idealism and His
    Transcendental Deduction." *Kantian Review* 20 (2015): 265–88.
Strawson, P. F. *The Bounds of Sense*. London: Methuen, 1966.
Van Cleve, James. *Problems from Kant*. Oxford: Oxford University Press,
    1999.
Willaschek, Marcus. *Kant on the Sources of Metaphysics*. Cambridge:
    Cambridge University Press, 2018.
Wimmer, H. and J. Perner "Beliefs about Beliefs: Representation and
    Constraining Function in Young Children's Understanding of
    Deception." *Cognition* 13 (1983): 103–28.
Wolff, Michael. "How Precise Is Kant's Table of Judgments?" In *Kant's
    Critique of Pure Reason: A Critical Guide*, edited by James R. O'Shea,
    83–105. Cambridge: Cambridge University Press, 2017.
Wood, Allen W. "The Antimomies of Pure Reason." In *The Cambridge
    Companion to Kant's Critique of Pure Reason*, edited by Paul Guyer,
    245–65. Cambridge: Cambridge University Press, 2010.
Wood, Allen W. *Kant*. Malden, MA: Blackwell, 2005.

INDEX OF CITATIONS OF PASSAGES IN THE *CRITIQUE OF PURE REASON*

Passages that occur only in A are listed by their pagination in A; all other passages are listed by their pagination in B. Entries for a range of pages sometimes include citations of pages within that range.

INDEX OF SUBJECTS
AND NAMES